Battleground General

Arnhem 1944

Battleground General

Arnhem 1944

Jon Sutherland and Diane Canwell

Pen & Sword
MILITARY

First published in Great Britain in 2011 by
Pen & Sword Military
an imprint of
Pen & Sword Books Ltd
47 Church Street
Barnsley
South Yorkshire
S70 2AS

ISBN 978-1-84884-484-1

A CIP catalogue record for this book is available from the British Library

Typeset in 11pt Ehrhardt by
Mac Style, Beverley, East Yorkshire

Printed and bound in the UK by
CPI

Pen & Sword Books Ltd incorporates the Imprints of Pen & Sword Aviation,
Pen & Sword Family History, Pen & Sword Maritime, Pen & Sword Military,
Pen & Sword Discovery, Wharncliffe Local History, Wharncliffe True Crime,
Wharncliffe Transport, Pen & Sword Select, Pen & Sword Military Classics,
Leo Cooper, The Praetorian Press, Remember When, Seaforth Publishing and
Frontline Publishing.

For a complete list of Pen & Sword titles please contact
PEN & SWORD BOOKS LIMITED
47 Church Street, Barnsley, South Yorkshire, S70 2AS, England
E-mail: enquiries@pen-and-sword.co.uk
Website: www.pen-and-sword.co.uk

Contents

How to Play *Battleground General*

Playing or reading *Battleground General* could not be easier. For the first time, you decide how the campaign progresses. You make the choices that would have been open to the generals in the campaign. You determine the outcome of the campaign by making the right choices at the right time. You finally get the chance to try out some of your own theories on how the campaign should have been fought.

After reading the opening entry, you will be given a series of choices. Each choice takes the story to its next logical phase. Simply turn to the new **Decision** number and continue to read the narrative and description of the outcomes of your choice. Keep reading and making choices until the campaign is won or lost. You can always choose the historical time line; *Battleground General* incorporates that into the choices offered. All of the other choices and their outcomes are speculative, based on what would probably have happened if the generals had chosen other courses of action.

You can choose either of the commanding generals, taking control of the action and determining the outcome of the campaign. Bear in mind, the book is designed so that the opposing general will try to out-think you; he will respond to your choices. Do not expect the opponent to give in easily; he will be aggressive at times, forcing you to react to his actions. When necessary, the opponent will be on the defensive and may try to extricate his forces before they are eliminated.

The storyline can either be played out to its logical conclusion, or it may end prematurely if a situation has developed where one side would naturally have decided to withdraw rather than face outright defeat and annihilation.

Introduction

On 6 June 1944, Allied forces landed on the beaches of Normandy. There was then a determined effort by the Germans to dislodge them, and a struggle lasting three months ensued. On 31 July, a coordinated Allied offensive broke out and swept across France. With British and Canadian forces in the north and US forces in the south, the bulk of the German Seventh Army was encircled and destroyed at Falais.

The German forces fell back in disarray, abandoning prizes like Paris that they had captured only four years before. Allied spearheads were advancing at a rate of 200 miles a week. By the beginning of September 1944, the bulk of France and Belgium had been liberated. Any day, Holland would be free, or so the Allies and the Dutch population hoped.

The truth was that the Allies had over-extended their supply lines. The remnants of the German Fifteenth Army still clung on to the French ports along the English Channel; supplies had to be driven up from Cherbourg and the Normandy beaches.

On 4 September 1944, the British 11th Armoured Division captured Antwerp. However, the approaches to the port were still in German hands. On the very same day, elements of the British Second Army were brought to a halt just miles from the Dutch border.

Lieutenant General Brian Horrocks, commanding the British XXX Corps, had his eyes on the capture of a Rhine River bridge into Holland. The river was the last major obstacle between the Allies and Germany itself. At this time, the Germans could barely muster a credible defence in this sector. Horrocks was certain that his tanks, fully-fuelled and with truck-loads of supplies on their way, could punch a hole through and be deep into Holland before the Germans could recover.

Meanwhile, German Army Group B, down to the bare bones following their losses in Normandy and in the retreat across France, began to improvise. By the time Horrocks was ready to advance again on 6 September resistance was stiffening. In the course of four days his men battered their way to seize two bridgeheads over the Meuse-Escaut Canal. Holland was just four miles away.

The Germans seized the opportunity of the temporary lull in offensive action at the beginning of September to extricate 82,000 men, along with their vehicles and artillery, over the Scheldt Estuary; the bulk of their Fifteenth Army would fight again.

The Allied Supreme Commander General Eisenhower was faced with a difficult decision on how to proceed. Field Marshal Montgomery commanding the British Twenty-First Army Group, the parent of the Second British Army, argued for all resources to be thrown into the effort to force an Allied path across Holland. Eisenhower was handed the details of Operation Comet, which planned to drop the British 1st Airborne Division across five key bridges around Eindhoven, Nijmegen and Arnhem. Horrock's troops would launch a ground assault to link up with the paratroopers and glider forces and thus punch a hole in the German defences as far as the Rhine. Operation Comet was to be launched on 9 September, but at the very last minute it was cancelled. It was simply too much to ask for a single airborne division to hold so much ground, albeit for a short period, until relieved by Horrocks.

The plan was not dead – unlike countless airborne operations that had been proposed and for various reasons cancelled since the airborne units had been used to such great effect in Normandy. A new mission, Operation Market Garden was born. Two additional divisions were added to the airborne side of the plan; the US paratroopers of the 82nd and the 101st Divisions. The new plan called on the 101st to take the bridges around Eindhoven; they could expect to be relieved by Horrocks in a matter of hours. The 82nd would land around Nijmegen; they could hope to be reached by XXX Corps in a day, perhaps two at the outside.

The British 1st Airborne Division with its 10,000 men, supported by 1,500 Polish paratroopers, would land around Arnhem. It was hoped that XXX Corps would reach them within three days.

If XXX Corps could get to Arnhem before the Germans destroyed the British paratroopers, then it was confidently expected that the war would be over by Christmas. The V2 rocket sites would be overrun, a push on Berlin itself launched or the industrial heartland of Germany, the Ruhr, captured.

It is the night of 16 September 1944, the day before the operation is to be launched. You can choose to take the role of Major General Robert 'Roy' Elliott Urquhart commanding the British 1st Airborne Division. Alternatively, you can opt to take the role of Obergruppenführer und General der Waffen-SS Wilhelm Bittrich commanding the II SS Panzerkorps , consisting of the 'Hohenstaufen' & 'Frundsberg' Divisions.

If you would like to play as Urquhart, turn over to page 1.

If you would like to play as Bittrich, turn to page 80.

Major General Robert Elliot Urquhart

In 1943, Major-General Hopkinson was killed in the early stages of the invasion of Italy. This left the 1st Airborne Division leaderless. Temporary command was given to Brigadier Eric Down, but he was sent to India to create a new airborne division.

One of the major problems in finding a replacement was the fact that there were few options within the small airborne force, so a man who understood how paratroopers would operate was necessary. Lieutenant General Browning, commander of the 1st Airborne Corps, chose Brigadier General Robert 'Roy' Urquhart. Urquhart was forty-three and after Sandhurst he had been commissioned in the Highland Light Infantry. Between 1941 and 1943, as a Lieutenant Colonel, he had commanded the 2nd Battalion of the Duke of Cornwall's Light Infantry, which was part of the 51st Highland Division serving in North Africa.

When Sicily and mainland Italy had been invaded, Urquhart had risen to the rank of Brigadier General and commanded the 51st Division's 231st Brigade Group. He was slightly wounded and was awarded the DSO and bar. Urquhart was then appointed to the General Staff of XII Corps of the Second British Army. Just a few months later, he was offered command of the 1st Airborne Division. He was shocked at the offer, believing the airborne corps to be a closed shop; he had no experience of this type of warfare. Urquhart realized that not only was this his opportunity to gain command of a division, but also that airborne troops, once dropped, were effectively ground troops which he had experience of handling.

Urquhart assumed command on 7 January 1944. Many of the senior officers and rank and file of the division were suspicious and sceptical of the appointment. In fact, one the brigadiers, Lathbury, had been given to understand, unofficially, that he would be given the division.

Urquhart faced a difficult time at first as Major General John Frost reported: '[Urquhart] was not a man to court popularity and, largely owing to the way the Division was dispersed all over Lincolnshire, we did not see him as much as we would have liked, but he very soon earned our complete respect and trust. In fact few generals have been so sorely tested and have yet prevailed.'

Urquhart quickly earned the respect of his men, as glider–pilot Sergeant Roy Hatch confirmed that Urquhart was 'a bloody general who didn't mind doing the job of a Sergeant'.

Urquhart now faced his greatest challenge: Operation Market Garden. The 1st Airborne had to land around Arnhem and then seize the river crossings, holding them until XXX Corps arrived. Urquhart knew that they were the end of the line; if anything went wrong and held up the armoured advance, the 1st Airborne would have to hang on.

During the planning for Market Garden, Urquhart regarded it as the job of an airborne commander to get hold of as many transport aircraft as possible without sparing a thought for the other Divisions involved, and so he made a habit of lodging frequent requests with Corps HQ. One time he asked for a further forty aircraft from Browning, who was doubtful that even a small number of these would materialize. Urquhart pointed out that the American Airborne Divisions were receiving more than their fair share of aircraft, but Browning dissuaded him from thinking that this had anything to do with American political pressure, and correctly explained that the divisions were given priority depending on how close they were to the starting line. The US 101st Airborne were to deploy almost all of their infantry strength with the First Lift, because to do otherwise would increase the possibility of a vital bridge being lost and those divisions to the north becoming cut off and utterly destroyed. On Friday 15 January, Urquhart was taking the opportunity to enjoy a round on the few holes still playable at Moor Park Golf Club, Corps HQ, when his Chief of Staff, Lieutenant Colonel Charles Mackenzie, put in an appearance to break the news that they were to lose some gliders on the First Lift. No explanation was given, but this was to enable Corps HQ to journey to Nijmegen. Urquhart insisted that whatever had to be left behind on the first day, anti-tank guns were not to be sacrificed. Despite the optimistic intelligence reports stating that there was no substantial German armour in the region to threaten them, Urquhart did not wish to take a chance.

Urquhart's 1st Airborne would be dropped some eight miles from their main objective, the bridge at Arnhem. From the outset, with just seven days to plan the operation, Urquhart faced strong opposition to operational changes from other commanders. He quickly realized that he would have to accept the situation and move on.

Urquhart was not a trained paratrooper. In fact, he suffered from air sickness. When he suggested to Browning that he ought to learn how to jump his Corps commander simply replied: 'I shouldn't worry about learning to parachute. Your job is to prepare this division for the invasion of Europe. Not only are you too big for parachuting but you are also getting on'. It was decided: Urquhart would land as a passenger on-board one of the gliders in the first lift.

Urquhart's Outline Plan

Urquhart gave his orders on the afternoon of 12 September 1944. In brief these were:

1. On the morning of 17 September, pathfinders of the 21st Independent Parachute Company (under Major B A 'Boy' Wilson) would land; they would mark out the three drop zones and landing zones for the first lift.
2. The major part of 1 Airlanding Brigade under Brigadier Philip 'Pip' Hicks would then arrive. They would secure the zones. Lathbury's 1 Parachute Brigade would strike for the railway bridge to the south of Oosterbeek, then the road bridge at Arnhem along with the pontoon bridge a further half-mile to the west.
3. Freddie Gough's 1st Airborne Reconnaissance Squadron would also be in the first lift; they would make the dash to seize the road bridge and hold it until 1 Parachute Brigade arrived.
4. Tactical HQ of the 1st Airborne, 1 Airlanding Light Regiment Royal Artillery (less a battery), 1 Airlanding Anti-tank Battery RA, the 1st Parachute Squadron Royal Engineers and other elements would also be in the first lift.
5. Johnnie Frost's 2nd Parachute Battalion was earmarked to relieve Gough first. It would take up positions on both banks of the Rhine. 3rd Battalion would then arrive and take up positions on the northern approach to the bridge. 1st Battalion would take the high ground to the north of Arnhem.
6. On 18 September, 4 Parachute Brigade would land and establish a defensive line to the north of the bridgehead.

7. On 19 September, the 1 Polish Independent Parachute Brigade would arrive, establish positions in the eastern suburbs of Arnhem and complete the bridgehead defensive ring.

8. 1 Airborne would then hold until relieved by the Second British Army.

Intelligence reports suggest that the flak around the Arnhem Bridge is heavy. The presence of German ground units is expected to be minimal. It is believed that there are six infantry divisions, twenty-five guns and around twenty tanks. The German troops are believed to be disorderly and dispirited.

The latest Dutch resistance reports on 15 September suggest that SS units have been seen in the Arnhem area. Urquhart was not given this information until after his division had landed.

If you wish to take on the role of Urquhart in the campaign, turn to **Decision 1**.

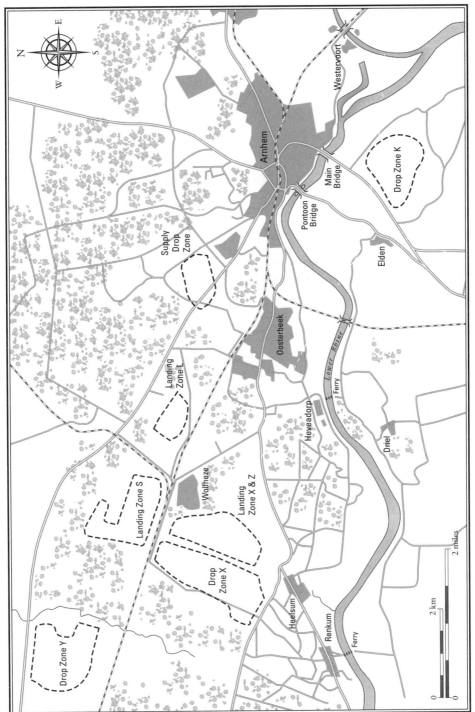

Urquhart's map.

Battleground General: Arnhem - British

1

Dawn: 17 September 1944

You are already wide awake before the sun comes up. Your batman, Hancock, is fussing about getting your uniform ready. Last night, in the fading light, you caught a glimpse of the tugs and gliders with freshly-painted white stripes across the wings and fuselages. The men were tense and eager for action.

The padre conducted an early-morning communion service on the airfield, and then you decided to eat alone in the mess. As you emerge the airfield in the West Country is buzzing with activity. The men look ready for anything, resplendent in their battle smocks and crash helmets and armed to the teeth. The men of the glider units are standing alongside their Horsas, and equipment is being loaded onto the Hamilcars, anti-tank guns and Bren gun carriers. You approach your own glider and see Graham Roberts, your ADC, Hancock, a signaller and a pair of military policemen who will be your escort and bodyguard.

Inside is your jeep and the policemen's motorcycles. It is a gloriously-sunny Sunday morning and the refreshment vans are doing a roaring trade. The men are reading the morning papers; some have chalked rude remarks on the sides of the gliders. You know this scene is being played out across dozens of airfields around England: revving engines, men savouring their last cup of tea, joking and wondering what the day will bring.

You decided that should the worst happen to you Brigadier Lathbury, commanding 1 Para Brigade, will assume command. With great trepidation you clamber aboard the Horsa. The glider is piloted by Colonel Ian Murray, commanding one of the two glider wings. Hancock has packed you a small shoulder pack with your shaving gear and other essentials. Clean clothes are in the jeep. You also carry a map of the Arnhem area, a notebook and a pair of grenades. Hancock eases your apprehension by chatting to you as you strap yourself in. Moments later there is a jolt as the tow-rope takes the strain. Feeling decidedly queasy throughout the flight, you are relieved that the journey is uneventful. Two enormous fleets of aircraft are *en route* to Holland; this time there are no last minute cancellations.

Glancing at your watch some time later you note that it is 1300. Boy Wilson's men will already be on Dutch soil. Half-an-hour later your glider lands gently and you jump out with Hancock by your side, leaving the others to unload the jeep. You stand for a while watching the near-textbook drop. Your staff are busying themselves setting up the tactical HQ under some trees at the edge of a wood.

If you want to remain at your HQ then turn to **Decision 26**. If you want to check on Hick's Airlanding Brigade to the north, of which there is no news at the moment, turn to **Decision 12**.

2

1800 hours 17 September 1944

You have barely covered 100 yards when you hear a terrific explosion off to your right. A huge plume of dust and debris blots out the darkening sky and the windows of the shops and houses shudder. You fear the worst but figure the explosion was too close to be the main road bridge at Arnhem. The Germans must have detonated charges on the railway bridge. You press on. There are definite signs of fighting along the streets. German and British bodies litter the pavements. Some of the buildings have obviously taken damage, but so far you have not seen a living soul. It is difficult to know exactly what you are driving into. If you want to proceed along the road, making for the main bridge, then go to **Decision 157**. If you want to take a turning to the right and head for the railway bridge then go to **Decision 28**.

3

The German tries the door. You can hear German voices outside. There is little time to make a decision. In seconds the Germans will be inside the house. If you want to stand and fight go to **Decision 168**. If you want to run out of the back of the house then go to **Decision 46**.

4

0600 hours 19 September 1944

You send Mackenzie to order Hackett to shift his line of attack and to push into Arnhem from the north-west. There is a real opportunity now to turn the tide of the battle, even if it means abandoning your original plans. With Lathbury pushing east through Oosterbeek, and Hackett threatening from the north, the Germans will be trapped in and around Arnhem. This is as long as you can protect your own northern flank. The Airlanding Brigade is still holding the drop zones, but is under constant pressure. If you want to retain them there then go to **Decision 48**. If you want to shift the whole division east then go to **Decision 102**.

5

'We'll hang on', you tell Frost and Gough.

They nod in agreement, but the situation looks pretty desperate. Throughout the day there are countless tank and infantry attacks on your perimeter. During the morning Frost is badly wounded in the leg. Tatham-Warner takes over, launching a series of counter-attacks to retake lost ground. And so it continues. By the end of 20 September it is clear that you cannot hold for much longer. Shortly before darkness, down to 130 men, you come under attack from Phosphor bombs and flamethrowers. This is the last straw; the flames are impossible to put out and you fear that the 200 or more wounded will be burned alive. There is no alternative but to surrender. Some of the men try to slip away in groups to the west to try and find the rest of the division. A ceasefire is negotiated and you reluctantly march into captivity.

6

You raise your hands in submission. There is no way out of the situation. You see the hull machine-gun of the tank covering your every move. You step out of the jeep, placing your pistol on the bonnet. The war is over for you. You can only hope that your division survives the battle without you.

7

You crouch down as Hackett sends a handful of men forward to investigate. All of a sudden a German machine gun opens fire, cutting down several of the men. Hackett screams the order to charge and bounds forward to engage the enemy. Now turn to **Decision 65**.

8

0900 hours 22 September 1944

You learn that the Germans have dubbed your defensive area 'the cauldron'. From your perspective it is indeed very hot. Your wounded are crowded into nine buildings, under constant mortar fire. The Germans are making increasing use of self-propelled guns, but your men are inflicting heavy casualties on anything that dares get close to your perimeter. You receive news that Horrocks has pushed the 43rd Division forward to link up with the Poles at Driel. You also hear that boats and rafts are being prepared and that contact should be made by tomorrow morning. Later you send off another signal: 'Perimeter unchanged. Positions heavily shelled and mortared during the day. Minor attacks defeated. Some SP guns knocked out. Assistance given by supporting artillery forward DIV. Intend ferry some Poles over tonight. Small attack direction ferry first light tomorrow. Morale high.'

You know it is going to be a hard day, but an idea begins to form. The longer you can remain on the north bank the more Germans will be employed trying to destroy you. If you could coordinate with the Poles and 43rd Division then a tenuous hold could be maintained, allowing amphibious crossings. If you want to suggest this idea then go to **Decision 108**. If you think it too late for any offensive action then go to **Decision 190**.

9

'Request Polish Brigade land shortly before dusk on DZK', you say in a signal to Corps. Almost immediately a signal comes back: 'Lead elements of XXX Corps 10 miles from your positions. Fog may well restrict Polish landing opportunities. Will confirm later.'

There is good and bad news here, but overall the situation is optimistic. If you want to go ahead with the operation and forget Polish involvement, then go to **Decision 128**. If you want to call it off go to **Decision 40**.

10

0600 hours 22 September 1944

During the night you are forced to commit 11 Para to the north to try and stem the tide of German assaults on the northern perimeter. Despite the prospect of XXX Corps being so close, you fear that the Germans will overwhelm you before they arrive. You realise that at this rate, feeding your battalions in piecemeal, they will be severely mauled and you will have little left to offer any resistance. You receive a signal just before midday: 'Lead elements XXX Corps at Elden. Request immediate attempt on southern bridge approach.'

If you want to comply with the order then go to **Decision 24**. If you think that it is impossible under the circumstances go to **Decision 146**.

11

1200 hours 21 September 1944

By noon you have affected several changes in your deployment. 1 and 2 Para hold the bridge approach, with 3 Para in reserve. 11 and 156 Para have shifted north to support Hackett. The KOSB hold the link between Hackett and the bridge. The Border Regiment protects the rear of the force in Arnhem. It is difficult to know if this will be enough. At 1300 Hackett signals that the landing zone has not yet been retaken. The Poles and the supplies could still be dropped, but there will be casualties. If you want to go ahead with the drop then go to **Decision 42**. Alternatively you could call off the drop at the last minute and go to **Decision 165**.

12

Preceded by the pair of military policemen, you head broadly north in your jeep. Hick's landing area is to the north of the railway line. So far you have seen no sign of the enemy, except for a handful of prisoners taken by Boy Wilson. You arrive at Hick's HQ without incident, only to discover that he is out visiting his battalions. Heartened by the news that his battalions have arrived in good order, you decide to head back towards your own HQ. Now go to **Decision 43**.

13

You clamber into your jeep with the signaller still trying to reach anyone on the radio. You drive down a cindered track and onto a secondary road. A few minutes later you are on the main Arnhem-Utrecht highway. You pass a private who is herding prisoners. From the shouted conversation you hear that Lathbury is in Oosterbeek, but that Frost is definitely on the southern route. If you want to make for Lathbury's HQ then go to **Decision 130**. If you want to change direction and make for Frost's battalion then go to **Decision 175**.

14

You spot Frost just up ahead. He is directing his men to converge on the approaches to the bridge. Joining him, you climb up stairs into a building on Markt Straat, which gives you a commanding view of the bridge. In the gathering darkness you can see a uniformed figure. Clambering down to the street a soldier rushes up to you and tells you that the figure was a Panzer SS man. The bridge is superbly designed, a great curving span, approached from the north by a vast concrete ramp.

'We saw German transports moving to the south moments ago', Frost tells you.

'Where's Gough?' you ask.

'He's over there', replies Frost, pointing at a waterworks building only fifty yards from the bridge.

'How many men have you got here?' you demand.

'About 500, spread out around the perimeter of the houses on this side of the bridge', Frost replies.

If you want to wait go to **Decision 122**. If you want to mount an assault on the bridge straight away then go to **Decision 58**.

15

0700 hours 18 September 1944

The Germans have been probing your positions all night. It has been virtually impossible to get any sleep. It does appear that the main German effort is to be mounted against the northern approach to the bridge. You have received reports of very little activity on the south side of the river. A dawn attack by a handful of German tanks, supported by Panzergrenadiers has been beaten off, but the casualties are mounting. You suspect that real trouble is brewing when the attack falters and there are several minutes of silence. Suddenly you hear the whine of shells and the impact of mortar rounds. The Germans begin plastering the defence perimeter all around the northern approach. A German reconnaissance unit bursts into view. It passes under the bridge ramp and breaks into Markt Straat. Your defences are thin and you fear they will break through. If you want to hold and fight them off then go to **Decision 187**. If you want to pull the troops back and over the bridge to the south end then go to **Decision 75**.

16

A Dutch naval officer, Lieutenant-Commander Wolters, had been loaned to the division a few days before the operation. He had, as planned, gone straight into Arnhem to ensure the liaison with the resistance and to feed back intelligence. Using the Dutch telephone exchange in Arnhem he has managed to get a message through. It is immediately relayed to you by one of your staff officers, Mackenzie:

'German tanks, about sixty of them, coming down the main road from Deelen airfield.'

'Are you sure?' you ask.

'Wolters is checking it, but we did have unconfirmed reports of a Panzer Corps refitting in the area.'

If you wish to stick to your decision and hold 4 Brigade back for now then turn to **Decision 150**. If you want to release them and push on into Oosterbeek then go to **Decision 115**.

17

In the afternoon Polish troops begin arriving on a landing zone between 10 Para and the Germans. The Germans open fire with flak, tracer, mortars and machine guns. The Poles, fighting for their lives as they land, accidentally mistake 10 Para for the enemy and open fire. 10 Para, licking its wounds, falls back to the Wolfhezen Crossing. Meanwhile, in Oosterbeek, the remnants of 1 and 2 Para, along with 11 Para and the South Staffords, have been in continuous action. Nearest the river the Germans have penetrated 11 Para's lines with tanks and self-propelled guns. Straggling groups of disordered and despondent paratroopers have been making their way back into Oosterbeek all day. There have been minor causes for celebration; two German tanks knocked out by Sergeant Baskerfield of the South Staffords. The unfortunate sergeant was killed in the action. Now turn to **Decision 33**.

18

'Fall back!' you shout, 'we can't hold them.'

You rush forward, waving the paratroopers back. In small groups they make the perilous dash to the reserve positions. Many of them are cut down by the concentrated fire of the German reconnaissance unit and their supporting infantry. Breathless, you flatten yourself against a wall. Frost looks utterly dejected.

'We've done our best', you tell him.

'Now we're cut off from the bridge and surrounded', he tells you.

'I know, but we're not done yet'.

Now turn to **Decision 103**.

19

'This is futile, we'll be overrun at any time', you tell Frost.

'Perhaps, but XXX Corps may be just a few hours from here', Frost argues.

'At least the Germans can't get troops across the bridge to engage XXX Corps', you concede.

'My thoughts exactly. Leave us here, we'll hang on for as long as we can. Just get the rest of the division moving', Frost pleads.

Reluctant to deplete Frost even further, you take just three men with you and strike west to find the lead elements of the division. Against the odds you manage to get through the German lines and are quickly updated. In places elements of the rest of the brigade have made some progress; Hackett's men have landed and have passed Oosterbeek and are threatening the German flank. They are under pressure from attacks from the north. Hackett's men have already penetrated the north-west of Arnhem but they are going south earlier than you had planned. If you want Hackett to keep north and approach Arnhem from that direction go to **Decision 124**. If you think he should act as he sees fit then go to **Decision 169**.

20

It was a good decision to stop where you were. Just 100 yards away you see a German Tiger tank lumber across the street and head north down a side road. It is followed by a half-track and a group of German infantry. It does appear that the Germans are pulling out of the area nearest the river after all. Perhaps there is hope you can break through to Frost. You wonder what the odds will be if you can consolidate near the northern approach to the bridge. Maybe you can hang on long enough for XXX Corps? Now turn to **Decision 126**.

21

'10 and 156 Para will hold SDZV for the time being', you tell your assembled officers. 'KOSB will provide a link between the landing zone and the main force in Arnhem.'

It is a good plan. It should work for the time being, but you doubt your chances of being able to hold the landing zone for very long. Now turn to **Decision 145**.

22

Your ADC Roberts, already hurt in the jeep crash, moves slightly by your side. A split second later he is hit by a sniper. With nothing else to be done aside from waiting for that inevitable bullet, you crouch and then break into a charge. Now turn to **Decision 127**.

23

0600 hours 25 September 1944

'We need to hang on for one more day. We'll collapse the perimeter tonight and make for the river. I'm afraid walking wounded only, the rest will have to stay.'

The officers look downcast and defeated, but still defiant, having held the Germans for days, outnumbered and out-gunned. Despite continued attacks during the day the perimeter stays largely intact. Increasingly, XXX Corps artillery is blunting German attacks. If only you had had this support a few days ago.

Nightfall brings your exit from the perimeter. It is very dark, with an inky sky, strong wind and heavy rain. Men drag themselves up from sodden ditches and begin to move south. Nearer the river the men hold hands or one another's smocks not to get lost. You leave in single file, making for the river bank and await your time for evacuation.

Eventually you are called over to a storm boat and make your way across the churning waters of the river. Even then you cannot rest; dawn is coming and there are still men under your command trapped on the northern bank. Over 10,000 of you dropped and just 2,163 will have returned.

24

'We've got to do it no matter what. Tell them to drop the Poles on DZK to support the attack.'

You decided to launch the attack, led by 1 Para, at 1000. You fear for the men, but as they approach the bridge ramp you are amazed that the Germans have failed to open fire. As the paras advance small groups of Germans appear from the superstructure of the bridge, their hands held high and some waving white flags. Your bold move was the last straw for them. Now turn to **Decision 41**.

25

The adjustments are made just in time, as the sky fills with allied aircraft and the drop begins. You watch in fascination as the Polish troops begin landing. They come under intense fire from the Germans, but Hackett has deployed his men so he can keep them at a reasonable distance. Once the Poles are down the Germans seem to withdraw; at least their fire is less intense. Perhaps they realise that it is too late for them? Hackett and the Poles collect the supplies together and await orders. If you want to continue to hold the drop zone go to **Decision 110**. If you think it is now pointless to do so then go to **Decision 182**.

26

As you walk over to the HQ you see a number of Dutch civilians wandering around. You surmise that they are patients from the nearby asylum. The signallers are trying to make their radios work but are finding it impossible to raise anyone. Your jeep is ready and offloaded. There is still no word from Hicks. If you wish to remain at the HQ go to **Decision 43**. If you want to check on Hicks go to **Decision 12**.

27

'We'll take our chance corporal', you reply, saluting the man.

'Very well sir, stick to the right of the road. The lieutenant colonel must be directing operations near the railway bridge.'

Gunning the jeep you speed forward. You have only covered a few yards when an ominous shape emerges from the side of the road. The silhouette is unmistakable. It is a German armoured car, swinging its main armament towards you as it gathers speed. If you want to put your foot down and speed past it then go to **Decision 112**. If you want to reverse out of trouble then go to **Decision 148**.

28

You cautiously edge down a side street, making for the river. As the remains of the railway bridge come into view you can see signs of heavy fighting. A flak emplacement shattered by rocket-firing Typhoons has dead German soldiers scattered around it. There are two or three wrecked enemy trucks standing abandoned with more dead, including paratroopers. The scene is otherwise deserted. Taking a last look at the remnants of the bridge you press on along the riverside road. Now go to **Decision 157**.

29

'Germans sir, heading this way!' shouts a paratrooper.

Immediately you hear the staccato bursts of a German machine gun. Abandoning the jeeps, you run. As you reach a side road Lathbury is hit and falls. Together with two other junior officers you pick him up and carry him into a house on Alexanderstraat. You lay Lathbury on the floor and check his wounds. It is not life threatening, but he has been partially paralysed by a bullet that has nicked his spine. He is bleeding but conscious, but you know he cannot travel any further.

'You must leave me here. It is no use staying. You'll only get cut off', Lathbury moans.

If you wish to leave him go to **Decision 132**. If you want to stay you should go to **Decision 59**.

30

Finally you are on the road and hoping to get a clearer picture of the situation. There seems to be a lot of movement on the side roads and you suspect it is the enemy rather than your own paratroopers. You have little time to waste and besides it would be dangerous to expose yourself. As you reach a bend in the road you spot Lathbury, who is making for your HQ. He flags you down and quickly explains that you were about to drive straight into a German unit just up the road. Now go to **Decision 29**.

31

It becomes obvious that the Germans have no idea where you are hiding.

'There's no future in this', you announce. 'We're contributing nothing.'

For now there is little you can do except to watch the Germans and hope that an attack from your troops breaks through to you. The day drags on as you await developments. Now turn to **Decision 133**.

32

1800 hours 18 September 1944

'Where the hell is XXX Corps! Not a peep and these damned radios are useless!' you rage.

The situation is getting out of control. As the minutes pass your forces weaken, whilst the Germans seem to be able to reinforce at will. Fragmentary reports from Arnhem suggest heavy fighting. A German attempt to rush the bridge with a reconnaissance unit was bloodily repulsed. You fear for Frost and what remains of his command. If the reports are correct then the planned drop zones for the Poles the next day will be a slaughter, as German armour is rumoured to be in the vicinity. Now turn to **Decision 143**.

33

2300 hours 19 September 1944

By the end of the day you find yourself in the uncomfortable position of having three separate commands. 2 Para and a company of 3 Para are desperately clinging on to the northern approach to the bridge. Elements of the 2nd South Staffords, 1, 3 and 11 Para are cut off in the Elizabeth Hospital area of Arnhem and the remainder of the division is to the west of Oosterbeek, with a tenuous hold on the landing zones. Your choices are becoming limited and it is difficult to tell how long Frost can continue to hold. The whole mission faces failure if the bridge is cleared by the Germans. Any prospects of XXX Corps arriving soon would be dashed. If you want to continue as you are and await developments then go to **Decision 161**. If you want to push east towards Oosterbeek turn to **Decision 105**.

34

'It's a pretty thin crust still sir', reports a sergeant from 11 Para as you approach the front line. 'They're still very aggressive and there's a number of tanks in the area roaming about. We can't do too much to stop them at the moment, lack of ammunition.'

You know this is a major problem, but pushing towards Arnhem still has to be the main effort. It worries you that the landing zones are compromised and this leaves you with the awkward situation of only having one landing zone, SDZV. This is near Lichtenbeek and is suitable for supplies only. The bulk of the Polish Parachute Brigade is still awaiting the chance to join the battle. Their intended landing zone, DZK near Elden on the south side of the river, is in German hands. You need to come up with a solution soon.

You pass through the western outskirts of Arnhem, keeping close to the river. Snipers are busy at work in the area, but so far you have not spotted any major German troop concentrations. If you want to drive on go to **Decision 151**. If you want to stop and bring up troops to take the ground you have already traversed then go to **Decision 20**.

35

You order the men to dig in and await news. From your vantage point you can see intense German activity in Arnhem. Hope is beginning to fade for any relief from the rest of the division. Radio contact is virtually non-existent. So far no serious German probes have been launched against your positions. It occurs to you that the Polish landings would be ideally placed around your positions, at least to strengthen your hold on the south end of the bridge. As long as you hold on to the southern exit the Germans cannot bring more troops to bear on XXX Corps. It is all that you can hope for at the moment. Now turn to **Decision 89**.

36

0600 hours 20 September 1944

You receive a call on the telephone: 'Hello Sunray', says the cheerful voice.

Suspicious that it might be the Germans, or that they may be listening in, you reply: 'Can you give me an inkling as to who you are?'

'It's the man who goes in for funny weapons', the voice replies; 'the man who is always late for your O groups.'

You remember that you had to discipline Gough about his poor punctuality during the planning of the operation.

'My goodness, I thought you were dead', you say.

Gough quickly explains that the situation at the bridge is precarious to say the least. The hold on the northern approach is weakening in the face of enormous German pressure. So far he has seen no signs of the Germans falling back as a result of your actions.

'It's pretty grim. We'll do what we can', Gough tells you.

You wish him the best of luck. If you want to press on with your attempts to break through then go to **Decision 171**. If you think it is too late and pointless then go to **Decision 125**.

37

1800 hours 20 September 1944

There has been no word from Hackett all day. At 1850 a small, mixed group of men stumble into your lines. Hackett has arrived with around thirty men from 156 Para, twelve from 10 Para, another dozen from his HQ, plus twenty other men and some officers. He has also scooped up sixty men; all sappers from the 4th Parachute Squadron. Hackett tells you of the struggles his men have had in order to get through to you. He sets up his HQ in the wooded part of the Hartenstein Hotel grounds, about 50 yards from your own HQ.

'Take a night's rest', you tell him, 'XXX Corps are still fighting in the Nijmegen area and are preparing to rush the bridge over the Waal'.

If you want to remain at HQ then go to **Decision 137**. If you want to check your perimeter, go to **Decision 38**.

38

In your jeep you make for Boy Wilson's Independent Company. His men are holding a number of houses in a heavily wooded area. On your way there you stray into no-man's land. A large number of SS men are moving into position to attack Wilson and you have arrived just at the wrong time. The road is too narrow to turn around, so you drive on towards the house you believe to be Wilson's HQ. Going fast you swerve to avoid a burned out German half-track, but you hit something and the jeep is thrown out of control. It hits a tree and is wrecked. Luckily you have been thrown clear. From the undergrowth you hear someone shout: 'For God's sake get out of it, snipers'.

If you want to obey the voice go to **Decision 78**. If you think it better to take cover where you are then go to **Decision 107**.

39

Attacks seem to be focusing on the south-east, north and north-east parts of the perimeter. Movement within the cauldron is very difficult; you can see from the men that they are exhausted due to lack of sleep and food. They have also been out in the open for days. Despite this their fighting spirit is still high. Attacks continue throughout the day. You realise there is little point in staying in position unless XXX Corps is making a determined effort to break through to you.

You send off a signal at 2015: 'Many attacks during the day by small parties infantry, SP guns and tanks, including flamethrowers. Each attack accompanied by very heavy mortaring and shelling within DIV perimeter. After many alarms and excursions the latter remains substantially unchanged, although very thinly held. Physical contact not yet made with those on south bank of river. Resupply a flop, small quantities ammunition only gathered in. Still no food and all ranks extremely dirty owing to shortage of water. Morale still adequate, but continued heavy mortaring and shelling is having obvious effects. We shall hold but at the same time hope for a brighter 24 hours ahead.'

If you now think it time to withdraw across the river whilst you still have men to command then go to **Decision 138**. If you would prefer to hold for another 24 hours turn to **Decision 79**.

40

As the day passes, with your men preparing for the attack, you receive disquieting news from Hackett. He has come against very determined attempts to dislodge him from the north of Arnhem and fears that he may not be able to hold. If you want to call off the attack and support Hackett then go to **Decision 80**. If you want to go ahead with the operation then go to **Decision 68**.

41

1200 hours 22 September 1944

You pull up the Border Regiment to support Hackett, leaving 1 Para in charge of the southern bank. 2 Para covers the northern approach and you are able to leave 3 Para in reserve. You venture across the bridge for the first time to witness the Polish landings. It is a sight you have dreamed of for several days. It is even better when you see tanks from the Irish Guards racing towards the landing zone. The whole area seems devoid of Germans, except for huge numbers of prisoners being scooped up by 1 Para. The operation has been a complete success. The final bridge is in allied hands. All that is left is for XXX Corps to get into Arnhem and help Hackett. Perhaps the war will be over by Christmas?

42

You drive up to personally witness the landings. Hackett is busy at work trying to consolidate as much of the landing zone as possible, but you can see the problems that he is facing. The Germans are bold, using self-propelled guns and tanks to rush your positions, slowly nibbling away at the perimeter of the landing field.

'This is going to be a massacre and you're to blame!' Hackett yells.
You forgive him for the moment, but there is a sneaking suspicion he may be right. If you want to get Boy Wilson to shift the drop zone flares to the south-east of the landing area then go to **Decision 25**. If you think things will be alright then go to **Decision 174**.

43

You wait for news. The first real information is not good. Freddie Gough's reconnaissance squadron, a mix of jeep-borne glider troops and parachutists, were supposed to deliver a *coup de main* against the Arnhem Bridge. The disaster has been that the gliders with most of their jeeps have failed to arrive. Your primary plan for the capture of the bridge has been scuppered at this early stage. With limited radio communication your options are limited. You desperately need to contact Lathbury and tell him that he is on his own. Ideally you should do it yourself, but whatever jeeps and men Gough can muster should precede you into Arnhem. You now have a major decision to make. If you want to send men out to find Gough then go to **Decision 56**. If you want to make for the Arnhem-Utrecht highway on your own and find Lathbury yourself then go to **Decision 70**.

44

1800 hours 17 September 1944

Reliable news is still scant. From what you understand Lathbury is still pinned down around Oosterbeek. There is no word of Frost, or of Lieutenant Colonel Dobie's 1st Battalion. The 1st Borderers are holding the Renkum and Heelsum area as ordered, protecting the rear. To the north the 7th King's Own Scottish Borderers are holding the northern approaches, along with the South Staffordshire Regiment. The second lift is due in the morning. It will bring you 4 Para Brigade, under Hackett, more anti-tank guns, artillery and the balance of the men that had to miss the first lift. As darkness is beginning to fall there are flashes off to the east and south-east. Occasionally you can hear the whine of shells. You can only hope that Lathbury has achieved his objectives. What is more, you fervently hope that XXX Corps is well on its way and is already at Eindhoven. Little more can be achieved tonight. Now go to **Decision 72**.

45

It feels good to be out on the road. The day is quiet so far. You make good headway and are on a bend in the road, just to the west of St Elizabeth Hospital, where the lower road meets up with the main road. Here you find Lathbury making for your HQ.

'Thank God I found you. If you'd continued up that road the Germans would have got you', Lathbury explains.

Now go to **Decision 29**.

46

You sprint out of the garden, turning right then left into another terraced house. A shocked Dutchman, Anton Derksen, points to the stairs. He tries to tell you that the Germans are coming. You pound up the staircase, almost too narrow for your boots. On the landing you pause and then enter a bedroom with a single wooden bed under the window. Glancing down to the street you can see several German soldiers and that you are opposite the hospital. The other officer, Cleminson, says, 'We can't get out this way. The place is crawling with them'.

If you want to try to shoot your way out then go to **Decision 114**. If you would prefer to wait go to **Decision 31**.

47

Accompanied by a strong force of mixed paratroopers, you head back towards Arnhem. Taking up a position in a tall house you carefully study the terrain, looking for German movement. It is becoming clear that the Germans are attempting to put a permanent wedge between you and Frost at the bridge. The Germans need to capture the bridge intact. This will allow them to slip armoured units south to block XXX Corps. At all costs this must be prevented. To achieve this, the Germans need to stop your advance, overwhelm Frost and then contain and defeat your division in detail. From your limited information you understand that Hackett is already running into heavy opposition in the north. Lathbury's forces are trying to push on a broad front, but encountering strong resistance. If you wish to continue the strategy as it is then go to **Decision 116**. If you wish to narrow your front by bringing Hackett further south and focus on breaking through to the bridge then turn to **Decision 186**.

48

Dobie's 1st Battalion and Fitch's 3rd Battalion have been attempting an advance towards Frost. Their approach has been made close to the river, under the cover of darkness and mist. Both battalions are barely worth the name, so decimated are they from the fighting. As they advance along the Ouderlangs, a flat road following a bend in the river near the harbour, they run into German defensive positions. As the mist clears the battalions are spotted by German units across the river, who add their fire. Dobie's battalion, or what is left of it, is decimated. The full weight of the German fire now falls on Fitch. His battalion is also cut to pieces and few of the men get out of the situation. Now turn to **Decision 88**.

49

The 11th Battalion suffers horrendous casualties in the fighting. You watch in horror as men stream back towards Oosterbeek. A 3rd Battalion officer, Dorrien-Smith, tells you:

'We'll have to pull out if this goes on. You'd better find somewhere for us to reorganise with the men we have left.'

By midnight you discover that the 3rd Battalion is down to forty men. Only 116 are left in 1 Para, 150 in 11 Para and the South Staffords are down to 100. Hackett still has 250 men of 10 Para and 270 of 156 Para. To the west, the Border Regiment is still holding on. Now turn to **Decision 188**.

50

You order a retreat south, heading for Elden on the road to Nijmegen. No sooner have you begun your retreat than the Germans launch an attack across the Arnhem Bridge, led by Tiger tanks and motorised infantry. It is a hopeless situation; your men hold them off for as long as their ammunition remains, but it becomes obvious that you will soon be overwhelmed.

'John, we need to end this', you tell Frost.

'Regrettably you're right', he replies.

With few men standing you send a paratrooper forward with a white flag. You and your men will spend the rest of the war in captivity.

51

From a brief telephone call from Gough at the bridge you learn that the situation for Frost's command is also dangerous. He tells you they will hold on as long as they can. You tell him that he can expect relief only from XXX Corps and that you are in no position to help. In fact you seriously doubt whether you can hang on for much longer. Now turn to **Decision 64**.

52

You move forward cautiously, but you are out in the open. Suddenly the unmistakeable sound of a German machine gun signals danger. Men are cut down around you. Hackett yells 'charge!' If you want to charge then go to **Decision 127**. If you think it more prudent to take cover then go to **Decision 65**.

53

You wait until darkness falls, coming under constant attack from the Germans. Snipers are everywhere and you barely dare to lift your head.

'Come on, we've got to get out of this', you decide.

The able-bodied men crouch, waiting for your signal.

'Charge!' you scream.

Now turn to **Decision 127**.

54

1900 hours 20 September 1944

Led by units of 1, 3 and 11 Para a firm connection has been made with Frost at the bridge. Hackett, with 10 and 156 Para, supported by the KOSB, have slipped into northern Arnhem and are holding the roads against increasing German pressure. The Border Regiment has moved up to take rearguard positions in a thin line to the west of Arnhem. If you want to consider the options for launching an assault on the southern side of the bridge go to **Decision 193**. If you would prefer to wait for news from XXX Corps then go to **Decision 119**.

55

1000 hours 22 September 1944

'Understand position. Poles will land to take southern approach, ETA noon', a signal informs you.

'Even if we can't commit to attack we'll support them as best we can', you tell your officers. 'Move up all artillery and bombard the southern approach to the bridge.'

You take up a good vantage point to watch operations. It takes half an hour to get the artillery into position and then they begin to open fire. You can also see fighting going on to the north of you. Hackett's men, even though you have supported them, are having a tough time; he needs to hold out. A few minutes before noon the sky is filled with aircraft and you begin to see Polish paratroopers floating down toward earth. The Germans are ready for them and it is a slaughter. In horror you avert your eyes. If only you had been bolder. Minutes later the Germans begin to withdraw. You can clearly see the lead units of XXX Corps arriving on the scene. Belatedly you order 1 Para across the bridge. There is little resistance from the Germans. The mission has been a success, but you regret not having had the courage to support the Poles. Their casualties were ruinous and unnecessary.

56

No one seems to know of Gough's whereabouts. Your signallers are still working hard to try to raise anyone on the radios. You feel very uneasy about the apparent disappearance of Gough. What is more, you feel cut off from events, with no idea how far the lead elements of Lathbury's brigade have penetrated into Oosterbeek and Arnhem. You saw jeeps speeding off, but most of the men were on foot. That was some two hours ago. You can only hope that Lathbury has seized the initiative and is close to the Arnhem Bridge. Now turn to **Decision 82**.

57

You climb aboard your jeep. The signaller is still trying to raise someone on the radio. From the expression on his face he is clearly having no luck at all. You drive down a cinder road towards the main Arnhem–Utrecht highway then make for a winding, cobbled road that seems to head down towards the river. So far you have seen little to suggest that there has been any fighting. But the ominous sound of gunfire and the crump of mortar shells is not far off. Now go to **Decision 140**.

58

'Let's not muck about, the bridge is what we're here for', you decide.

'But the Germans know we're here', replies Frost.

'It's a risk but this might be our best chance', you answer.

Frost nods his assent and then begins the process of warning the men and organising the attack. You can make out what appears to be a line of wooden huts on the bridge. They are on the western side, each about 20ft in length. In front of them is a pillbox firing at shadows and keeping the men's heads down. If you want to try to deal with the pillbox first go to **Decision 141**. If you prefer that the assault goes ahead you should turn to **Decision 85**.

59

'We need to stay here and make sure he gets proper medical attention', you tell Taylor, an intelligence officer on Lathbury's staff.

'That's not wise sir', Taylor replies.

'Go, leave me, the Germans will take care of me', Lathbury adds.

Suddenly you see a German peering into the room from the window. If you wish to fire at him go to **Decision 142**. If you think the game is up and want to surrender go to **Decision 123**.

60

1800 hours 18 September 1944

Fragmentary and contradictory reports filter in all evening. In places Lathbury has made good progress but in others his advance has stalled. Hackett's men have nearly passed Oosterbeek, threatening the German flank, but they are coming under pressure from German thrusts from the north. Hackett's lead units are already in the outskirts of Arnhem, further south east than you had wished. If you wish to order Hackett to keep north and approach Arnhem from that direction then go to **Decision 125**. If you are content for him to act as he sees fit under the circumstances then go to **Decision 169**.

61

From reports it seems that the Polish landings have gone ahead. Clearly the message you sent about the changes to the drop zones did not get through. Luckily they have landed in good order, as the Germans have shifted their strength to follow the tail of Hackett's men pushing into Arnhem. The pressure from Hackett allied with the continued push from Lathbury's men has squeezed the Germans sufficiently for them to withdraw to the north and away from the river. At 1800 you are cheered by the news that 3 Para and elements of 1 Para have linked up with Frost. It seems that they have moved in the nick of time; by dark the majority of your division has pushed into Oosterbeek, or are holding positions in Arnhem. German resistance in a number of areas is still strong. If you want to remain at HQ then go to **Decision 189**. If you want to drive into Arnhem and find Frost then turn to **Decision 34**.

62

0900 hours 18 September 1944

'Vehicle engines to the south sir', reports a sergeant.

'What are they, XXX Corps?'' you demand, peering through your binoculars and desperately trying to see the vehicles.

'I thought I saw a Humber armoured car sir', the sergeant adds.

'Thank God: it's XXX Corps', Frost shouts.

The bridge begins to vibrate. You can hear tracks rattling and screeching. The column is heading your way.

'Can you see anything?' you ask Frost. You are unable to make anything out, as the lead vehicle has not yet reached the centre of the bridge. Your question is answered as the shape of a German Puma armoured car appears, firing its main armament and machine gun. Two more armoured cars emerge and speed straight down the ramp and into the town centre. Three more appear, but one hits the mines on the bridge. It bounces away from the explosion and starts belching smoke and flames. If you want to try and hold them, go to **Decision 144**. If you want to fall back into Arnhem you should turn to **Decision 117**.

63

Led by Tiger tanks and supported by half-track-borne infantry, the Germans swarm across the Arnhem Bridge. Your PIATs and a single anti-tank gun prove useless against the armour of these monsters. At any moment the full weight of the German attack will overwhelm you. You order all able-bodied men to make for the south as quickly as they can. Hopefully some will make it back to allied lines. You stand amongst your wounded and await the inevitable capture and failure.

64

10 Para is the first to try to break through to you. By the time you see their commander, Smyth, the unit has been reduced to around sixty men.

'What's happened to Hackett?' you demand.

'I hope he'll be here soon, providing he can disengage', he replies.

The situation has taken another turn for the worse. There is little hope now and your chances of establishing a perimeter will be even less likely if Hackett is lost. If you want to wait for Hackett and concentrate on the perimeter then go to **Decision 37**. If you want to try and help Hackett to get out of the situation then turn to **Decision 192**.

65

You hit the dirt as machine-gun bullets rake the earth around you. Hackett hares off after the Germans. The enemy swiftly retreats at the sight of the onrushing paratroopers. They take cover in a shallow depression, but Hackett's men root them out and occupy the position themselves. You join him, quickly realising that the place is a death trap. Now turn to **Decision 194**.

66

It is an ignominious end to the operation. You manage to get nearly 2,000 men back across the ferry to the south side of the river. Here you have an equally-challenging task, but eventually fight your way south towards XXX Corps, who have raced up the road from Nijmegen to relieve you. Hackett was left behind on the other side of the river after the ferry was captured by the Germans.

'Indecision and lack of courage', Hackett would later write in his memoires. You feel that the criticism is unfair. Nonetheless the operation was a failure and you shoulder the blame like any commander should.

67

'We take the opportunity to move south during the lull in the firing. We collapse the perimeter in the north and re-establish to the south.'

The plan works to perfection, except the ferry at Heveadorp remains in German hands. The Poles attempt a crossing to dislodge them but they are thrown back with heavy casualties.

Your perimeter, thinly held, is now centred around the river bank and the southern outskirts of Oosterbeek. At 1900 hours, with your men digging in around the new perimeter, you receive a signal from Browning: 'You are to organise evacuation as soon as practicable. XXX Corps will support your withdrawal with all available artillery. Consider your best option is cover of darkness September 25.'

Now turn to **Decision 23**.

68

2200 hours 21 September 1944

'We go ahead tonight', you decide, knowing that the situation is grim in the north, but also realising that the sooner you make a junction with XXX Corps the better.

By midnight 1 Para is in position, with 3 Para in reserve. The night is pitch black and ideal for the operation. You stare in awe as the lead company of 1 Para creeps onto the bridge. You expect there to be firing at any minute, but there is silence for several minutes. More companies move forward. You hear sporadic firing towards the far end of the bridge. You can hardly believe your luck; you wait with bated breath for the green signal to be fired. After an eternity the light arcs into the night sky. The bridge has been taken. Now turn to **Decision 155**.

69

0600 hours 21 September 1944

A confirmation signal has informed you that the Poles, along with supplies, will land at SDZV at 1700 today. Events of the morning, however, are most alarming. Hackett's troops have come under heavy pressure from mixed units of Germans, supported by tanks and self-propelled guns. In a snatched conversation by radio Hackett tells you he has had to fall back from part of the landing zone and needs at least two additional battalions to re-establish his control of the area. If you want to send him reinforcements then go to **Decision 11**. If you think he is over reacting then go to **Decision 95**.

70

You clamber into the jeep with your signaller on the back seat, still trying to raise someone on the radio. As you roar off you shout to your staff, instructing them to tell Gough, should he be found, that he is to contact you immediately at Lathbury's HQ. From your limited understanding Lathbury is following John Frost's 2nd Battalion on the Low Road towards Arnhem. You make the decision to follow that intelligence, presuming that Frost is making directly for the bridge. You drive down a cindered track and onto a secondary road. A few minutes later you reach the main Arnhem-Utrecht highway. It is a modern road fringed with trees. There are wide avenues between the conifers on the roadside and you can see the prosperous homes of Dutch civilians. A minute or so later you spot a line of dishevelled Germans being herded towards the landing zone by a solitary paratrooper. If you want to stop and talk to the paratrooper go to **Decision 96**. If you want to drive on go to **Decision 147**.

71

'Keep pressing Gerry', you tell Lathbury. 'Make every effort to support Frost and for God's sake link up with 1st Battalion. Hackett's men will be here in the morning and I'll make sure you get every man I can spare. The main effort is here.'

Lathbury orders a signaller to take your man's place and you head off towards the HQ, retracing the route you took earlier. Now go to **Decision 44**.

72

0600 hours 18 September 1944

Today's news is alarming. The Germans have reinforced their lines around Oosterbeek during the night. To the west and north German forces have been probing the landing zones' perimeter defence lines all night. This was not what you were given to expect at all. Still, the principal priority is to seize the bridges. That is as long as they have not been destroyed. Equally, fresh troops will begin arriving today. At the very least it will ease the pressure on the men, who have already been in combat for nearly eighteen hours. A worrying sign is the occasional but increasing numbers of German shells landing around the HQ area. You understand from reports that Lathbury has made intermittent contact with Frost. The railway bridge has been destroyed by the Germans. Frost's attempt to seize the road bridge has stalled, but he holds the northern approaches with a few hundred men. If you want to remain at HQ then go to **Decision 84**. If you want to drive and consult with Lathbury then go to **Decision 45**.

73

Patiently waiting for developments, your forward positions report that they can hear traffic on the south side of the bridge. As far as you are concerned it is bad news. But one hopeful paratrooper calls out, 'It's XXX Corps!' You seriously doubt his optimism.

Frost's men are in good defensive positions around the northern end of the bridge. Peering through your field glasses you are sure that the approaching vehicles are trucks. Suddenly, all hell breaks loose, as flamethrowers and anti-tank weapons engage the convoy.

'German trucks!' shouts Frost. 'They can't know we're here, pour it into them!'

The ambush is a slaughter. The half-dozen lorries packed with unsuspecting Germans are caught in a lethal cross-fire. In a matter of moments the carnage subsides, leaving enemy dead and wounded littered all over the bridge. If you want to seize the opportunity and launch an assault now then go to **Decision 85**. If you would rather wait for developments then turn to **Decision 176**.

74

Progress is a little better as you commit more troops to the fighting in Oosterbeek. It is still too slow, however, and you consider your options. Until Hackett's men arrive you have limited resources. But the battle needs to be fought in Oosterbeek and then Arnhem and not around the landing zones, no matter how precious they are now. After Hackett has arrived with 4 Parachute Brigade you could divert the Polish landings and drop them to support your push on the south side of the bridge. Now turn to **Decision 184**.

75

'Retreat over to the south side of the bridge!' you shout, figuring that if you hold the south approach to the bridge then XXX Corps can still link up with you. There might be a possibility that the rest of your division can take the northern approach back. Gough's reconnaissance unit leads the way over the bridge and under severe pressure you filter your men back across the bridge, retreating in companies as the Germans harry your every move. Casualties are high; some of your men are cut off. By the time you reach the south end of the bridge your command is down to less than 300 men. The Germans are already trying to force the bridge from the north. If you want to try to dig in and defend the bridge then go to **Decision 160**. If you wish to send what remains of Gough's unit south to link up with XXX Corps then turn to **Decision 35**.

76

'We need to break out and link up with the division', you tell Frost and Gough, at a hastily convened staff meeting.

'We'll never make it, and besides XXX Corps could be here any time soon', Frost disagrees.

'Perhaps, but I've made my decision. We'll fold up the defences carefully; pull back the men from the eastern side of the approach first. Gough will then lead a probing attack west. We keep moving as best we can to the west, until we reach our lines.'

Now turn to **Decision 135**.

77

As the day progresses the news from Hackett is bad. His brigade has taken huge losses in continuing to press forward. The Border Regiment to the west has lost contact with you. 156 Para has been badly mauled, Hackett was forced to switch the spearhead unit, putting 10 Para at the point. Towards midday you see 10 Para's commander, Lieutenant Colonel Smyth. He is wounded in the arm.

'I have sixty men left', he tells you.

'What's happened to Hackett?' you ask.

'He'll be here soon, that's if he can disengage', he tells you.

The offensive is over. There is nothing for it now but to try to create a perimeter and hold on as long as possible. If you want to get to Hackett and help him then go to **Decision 192**. If you would prefer to wait for him and organise your perimeter then go to **Decision 37**.

78

Your ADC Roberts is hurt in the leg, but together you manage to jump over a 4.5ft wire mesh fence and get to the house. Presently, the firing dies down and you are safe to leave and head back to HQ. Your jeep is a write-off. Now go to **Decision 137**.

79

0600 hours 24 September 1944

Through Graeme Warrack, your chief doctor, you agree to allow the bulk of the badly wounded to be handed over to the Germans for treatment. Hackett will be one of these men; he has been badly wounded in the thigh and stomach by a mortar round. No sooner has the evacuation taken place in the afternoon than the Germans renew their attacks. By evening the perimeter is still largely unchanged. You receive a signal from Browning. It is clear from the message that it is Browning's view that you now evacuate. He tells you that 130 Brigade, along with the Poles, will attempt a crossing near the Heveadorp ferry. The best this can achieve is to cover your withdrawal. Now turn to **Decision 109**.

80

'Shift the South Staffords to support Hackett. The operation is off for now', you order. 'New priority for the time being is to hold what we have. XXX Corps is close. With luck they'll be within striking distance of here by midday tomorrow.'

The men are disappointed but given the ferocity of the fighting to the north there is no real option. The Germans have thrown Tiger tanks, self-propelled guns and masses of infantry into attacks and Hackett is hard pressed to hold. Now turn to **Decision 120**.

81

'Must insist on new plan as per my requests. Feel that Polish Parachute Brigade more valuable north of bridge. Constant pressure from German attacks today. Will need reinforcement to ensure our bridge remains open for now', you reply.

Now turn to **Decision 69**.

82

Kicking your heels, you wait impatiently for news. The first you hear is of the opposition your men are facing at Oosterbeek. A handful of prisoners have been herded back to the landing zone. They look surprisingly young and fit. More alarmingly, you discover that they are SS Panzergrenadiers. You quickly learn that they are part of a depot and reserve battalion commanded by an SS captain, Sepp Kraft. There are also rumours that some of the paratroop battalions are running into elements of the 9th SS Panzer Division 'Hohenstaufen'. As far as you can gather Frost's battalion is continuing its advance but the two other lead battalions are blocked by enemy units. If you want to remain at the HQ go to **Decision 111**. If you now want to check the situation for yourself and update Lathbury then go to **Decision 70**.

83

1800 hours 17 September 1944

'Gerry, we must keep pushing forward. Heaven knows how close Frost is to the bridges. 1 Para needs to be protecting your flank to let 3 Para push on', you tell Lathbury.

'Agreed, but it worries me that we are running into SS and not reserve troops. They also seem to have a handful of vehicles too. There are rumours of armoured cars, tanks and half-tracks moving into Oosterbeek," he tells you.

'So much for the ear-and-stomach battalions eh? You didn't believe that for a minute did you', you reply.

You duck as another mortar stonk straddles the wood and crossroads. 'Push on until dark', you conclude.

Now go to **Decision 131**.

84

The troops around the landing zones have had a sleepless night. They have been under attack. You understand from captured Germans that the night attacks in the west are being coordinated by Von Tettau, commanding a mix of defence and training units. From the east, and more ominously, the 9th SS, under Harzer, have been pounding your positions. Hick's 1 Airlanding Brigade have had no other option but to dig in. So far there is no word from the units attempting to break through to the Arnhem Bridge, but a tenuous link has been established with Frost himself. You are waiting impatiently for the arrival of today's airborne reinforcements. You cannot help gazing to the south for a sign of XXX Corps. If you want to talk to Frost on the radio go to **Decision 99**. If you want to drive forward and find Lathbury then go to **Decision 30**.

85

You signal to Frost to launch the attack on the bridge. Seconds later, waves of men surge forward. They come under immediate fire from the Germans, but it is hard to make out what is happening. Mortar bombs land around the approaches to the bridge. You can hear shouts and grenades exploding. The armoured car has reappeared and is firing. A moment later a PIAT silences the vehicle. There is a cheer and the men press forward with renewed vigour. Resisting your own urge to move forward, you watch the grim spectacle, proud of your men.

'We're halfway across. The Germans are pulling back!' shouts Frost.

'Press on, seize the southern approach!' you yell back to him.

He disappears into the darkness. Your key first day objective has been taken. All you can hope is that XXX Corps are as good as their word and get here tomorrow. During the night you also need the rest of the brigade under Lathbury to press on and link up. Perhaps the operation will be successful after all. Now go to **Decision 113**.

86

'Hang the drop-zones to the north of the railway, we'll concentrate here. Get a message to Boy Wilson and his men to put the markers out around the main drop-zones. Get Hackett to land here', you order the radio operator.

Shortly afterwards you hear disturbing news. The second lift has been delayed. The skies above Arnhem might be bright and clear, but in England there is low cloud and fog. With painstaking care you begin to send out orders for a withdrawal from Drop Zone Y and Landing Zone 5. The news of the delay makes this even more imperative. Now go to **Decision 184**.

87

As you make slow progress east you realise that if anything the number of Germans moving up is increasing. There seems to be significant forces between Lathbury and Frost. At times you are forced to hide in gardens and houses for several minutes as German units pass you. Cleminson and Taylor, the two officers with you, are uncertain about your chances of getting to the bridge. Keeping to the south, nearest the river, you are suddenly challenged. It is an English voice. Shouting back you find yourself amongst C Company of the 3rd Battalion. Major Lewis is pleased but surprised to see you.

'We've orders to find a route through to the bridge', he explains.

'Just where we're heading', you answer.

'We've just cleared a small German group sir and we're pushing forward if you'd like to join us.'

By dusk you are in the heart of Arnhem. It is deserted and eerily silent. From the railway station you move cautiously through narrowing shopping streets, ever alert for snipers. Up ahead some of Lewis's men have just knocked out a German armoured car with a gammon bomb.

'It's the bridge sir, we've just made contact with 2 Para,' a breathless corporal explains.

Now turn to **Decision 101**.

88

Luck has not been on the side of the 2nd South Stafford's side either. By 0800, under intense fire from the Germans, their advance has come to a halt. By 1100 you hear that they have reached the Municipal Museum in Arnhem. They are now under attack from German self-propelled guns and infantry. The battalion lacks any real anti-tank weapons. If you want to reinforce them with the 11th Battalion then go to **Decision 49**. If you want to order them to hold then go to **Decision 179**.

89

0900 hours 19 September 1944

'Sir, we've got radio contact with XXX Corps', shouts an excited signaller.

'Where are they?' you demand.

'South of Nijmegen, they're on the outskirts.'

'There's little hope then', you reply.

The Germans seem to be massing on the northern approach to the bridge. You fear that they will launch an assault and overrun you. It is pointless trying to imagine that the Poles can be dropped in time. If you want to remain in position then go to **Decision 63**. If you want to pull back along the road to Nijmegen then go to **Decision 50**.

90

A wounded Lieutenant Colonel Ken Smyth finds you. He is the commander of 10 Para. Trailing along the road behind him is what remains of his battalion; just 60 men.

'What happened?' you ask.

'We've tried everything. Hackett is trying to disengage.'

If you want to try and help Hackett then go to **Decision 192**. If you want to try and organise a new perimeter defence turn to **Decision 37**.

91

You quickly realise the cost of your decisions are being paid by your men. Casualties continue to mount and further forward movement is becoming impossible. Now turn to **Decision 188**.

92

'I've made my decision. It hasn't been an easy one to make, but if any of us want to get out of this alive we need to withdraw now', you begin.

From the expression on your officers' faces this is not a popular decision.

'We've no hope of breaking through to Frost; XXX Corps is unlikely to get here any time soon; we've got 3,000 men left standing out of 10,000; and by this time tomorrow we could be overrun.'

'But the mission! The whole point of the sacrifices and the casualties. We've been training for this sort of operation for months', Hackett replies.

Other officers murmur their support of Hackett's view. If you want to stick to your decision to withdraw then go to **Decision 66**. If you want to change your mind then go to **Decision 173**.

93

0600 hours 24 September 1944

By the early hours around 200 Poles have reached your perimeter. Hackett, on his way back from positioning the Poles, has been caught by a mortar round and has been wounded in the stomach and thigh. Graeme Warrack, your chief doctor, is very concerned about the wounded. You can see that he has something on his mind: 'If you don't mind I would like to go and see the German commander and arrange for the evacuation of our wounded to his hospitals in Arnhem', he asks.

You are concerned that this would give out the wrong messages and that the Germans will think you are on the verge of collapse.

'Alright, you may make the attempt on condition that the Germans understand that you are a doctor representing your patients and not an official emissary from the division,' you tell him.

After a time Warrack comes back. The Germans have agreed. They will slacken their fire in the afternoon to allow the evacuation and Hackett will be one of them. If you want to take the opportunity of the reduction in fire to realign your perimeter further south and closer to the river then go to **Decision 67**. If you think that this is not in the spirit of the agreement, then go to **Decision 164**.

94

'Request Polish landings at SDZV. Urgent need for additional anti-tank guns, PIATs and ammunition', you say in your signal.

You wait for the best part of three hours for a reply.

'Understand only this drop zone under your control. Request you abandon this drop zone and focus on Arnhem bridgehead. Primary objective remains the southern approach to facilitate link up with XXX Corps.'

The instructions seem pretty clear. If you want to follow the orders and abandon the landing zone then go to **Decision 193**. If you want to insist your new plan is implemented then go to **Decision 81**.

95

'Just retake the landing zone. Is that understood?' you tell Hackett in a terse conversation over a faltering radio set.

'I'm not sure I can do it. The Germans have dozens of tanks here. They are in amongst my lines and the artillery and mortar fire is breaking up our counter-attacks.'

He could be right after all. If you want to send him reserves then go to **Decision 11**. If you want to order him to withdraw and call off the drop then go to **Decision 165**.

96

1530 hours 17 September 1944

The paratrooper, a private, swings his Sten towards your jeep. As soon as he realises who you are he smiles and snaps to attention. He tells you that the Germans were captured on the outskirts of Oosterbeek. Two of the paratroop battalions are facing increasing resistance and have made little headway. The soldier has no idea how Frost is progressing, but believes him to be on the road closest to the lower Rhine, making for the Arnhem railway bridge, the first objective. If you wish to head for Oosterbeek then go to **Decision 130**. If you want to find Frost's battalion on the southern road and to the east of Oosterbeek then go to **Decision 175**.

97

Ordering Lathbury to keep pressing forward and to link up with Frost's 2nd Battalion and Dobie's 1st Battalion, you head south, eventually reaching a row of shops. You see some more bodies here, then you spot a paratrooper anti-tank gun being pulled into the window of a wrecked shop. Suddenly a corporal waves you down.

'Jerry is up ahead. An armoured car. We've laid a trap for him. You should get off the road sir', he explains.

'Where is Lieutenant Colonel Frost?' you demand.

'No idea sir, we're part of the rear company. I suspect he is making for the railway bridge. I'd really urge you not to proceed along the road', he tells you.

If you want to take the corporal's advice then go to **Decision 166**. If you want to drive on and find Frost then go to **Decision 27**.

98

0300 hours 18 September 1944

You are roused early and after quickly getting ready you emerge onto the road. Accompanying you is 3rd Battalion's RSM, a huge man called Lord.

'From now on sir, I'm your bodyguard', he tells you.

You have realised that it is pointless being involved in a battalion-sized action when there is the rest of the division to consider. It is still not daylight but this could be your last good chance to get back to HQ. Alternatively you could try to make it to Frost, who must be at the bridge by now. If you want to head for HQ then turn to **Decision 29**. If you wish to try to break through to Frost then go to **Decision 183**.

99

'John', you begin, 'So sorry about all of this. You're on your own for now. We're trying to break through to you but the Germans are reinforcing far quicker than we had anticipated.'

'I understand. We're holding the northern approach, but we're too weak to try and take the bridge', he explains.

'Just hang on John, we're coming. The second lift is due soon. That should tip the balance', you try to reassure him.

'XXX Corps?' Frost asks.

'No word. Communication is fragmentary at best, sorry'.

The connection is severed and you slam down the handset in disgust. If you want to concentrate your efforts now on protecting the landing zones go to **Decision 86**. If you want to redouble your efforts to break through to Frost then go to **Decision 158**.

100

You dodge into some gardens to avoid a group of German soldiers moving in your direction. You hear them trudging past, clearly in high spirits. You continue making your way west. Finally you run into a mixed-group of South Staffords and men from the 11th Battalion. They tell you that Hackett has arrived but has not yet been fully committed. The HQ has been set up at the Hartstein Hotel in Oosterbeek. You quickly relay the intelligence you have on German troop movements to the officer in charge and head for the HQ to get a better picture of the overall situation. Now turn to **Decision 159**.

101

With incredible care you manage to make it through to Frost. He is delighted to see you. Quickly he updates you on the situation. His battalion holds the main approach to the north side of the bridge. But he is contemplating an all-out assault on the bridge itself. A decision has to be made about this, particularly as there is no immediate prospect of reinforcement. Now turn to **Decision 73**.

102

1800 hours 19 September 1944

Your move to the east seems to be paying off to some extent. Elements of the 2nd South Staffords, 1, 3 and 11 Para are fully established in the Elizabeth Hospital area of Arnhem. Hackett's men are moving on the Arnhem Bridge from the north. You have collapsed the rear of your perimeter and most of the men are heading into Oosterbeek. The Germans have responded by overrunning most of the landing zones. This now presents you with another problem; that of resupply. Your only viable supply drop lies to the north east of Oosterbeek, near Lichtenbeek. This needs to be held at all costs. It is believed to be unsuitable for airborne reinforcement and your understanding is that the intended drop for the bulk of the Polish Parachute Brigade, DZK, near Elden, is already overrun by the Germans. A garbled message from XXX Corps indicates that they have reached Nijmegen and are attacking the road and railway bridges. Now turn to **Decision 36**.

103

German infantry, self-propelled guns and tanks are close behind. Ahead of you the exit seems clear, but you know it is fraught with danger. What remains of Frost's command is now on the western edge of the northern approach to the bridge. The situation is grim. For several minutes you ponder your options.

'You should get out now sir, at least you could try and coordinate a breakthrough to us', Frost suggests.

You feel he is right, but it would mean perhaps abandoning Frost to his fate.

'Alright, maybe the rest of the division isn't far from here. The bridge worries me now John. The Germans can push what they want across it.'

'We'll see about that, now get moving. We'll hang on as long as we can', he shouts.

Now turn to **Decision 100**.

104

0900 hours 19 September 1944

There is still no word from XXX Corps, or from Gough. Your scouts report elements of the 10th SS massing to the east, but they appear to be heading in the direction of Nijmegen. German units seem to now be concentrating on the northern approach to the bridge and you are sure that an attack is imminent. If you want to remain in position then go to **Decision 63**. If you want to pull back along the road to Nijmegen then go to **Decision 50**.

105

'We need to collapse the perimeter in the west and push eastwards', you tell your staff.

'How? It is too late for that. The Germans are in significant strength ahead of us and to the north', one of your officers argues.

'I know that. But surely we can break through', you argue back.

'Maybe, but at what cost?' another officer adds.

'As things are they'll pick us off in detail; Frost first then the boys in Arnhem and then us. Let's get ourselves firmly established in Oosterbeek, abandon the landing zones and see what can be done.'

Now turn to **Decision 188**.

106

You slide the jeep into reverse and slam your foot down, speeding backwards and away from danger. It is a tricky manoeuvre; keeping an eye on the German tank and the peril of rubble and debris on the road. The German tank gives up the chase and there is no sign of the half-track. Maybe there is a chance you can break through to Frost this way. Now turn to **Decision 126**.

107

Within seconds you hear bullets pinging around you. One smacks into a nearby tree, missing you by inches. A second ricochets off the wrecked jeep. Any minute now the German snipers will seek you out. If you want to run for the cover of the house then go to **Decision 78**. If you think it better to wait then go to **Decision 22**.

108

0600 hours 23 September 1944

You decide to send a signal to Corps, telling them of your intentions: 'Under cover of mist intend to contract perimeter's northern line and move remaining units south to retake ferry and establish positions around river bank. Move will take place at 1000 hours. Request artillery support and demonstration on south bank as diversion. Request DUKWs to bring Poles and supplies once established. Estimated to be complete 1200.'

Several minutes later you receive a reply: 'XXX Corps diverted brigade to Veghel to counter German attempt to cut corridor. Limited resources available nonetheless concur with your plan. All possible assistance will be given.'

Now turn to **Decision 196**.

109

'We leave tonight under cover of darkness', you tell your assembled officers. 'Just one more day.'

The officers look downcast and defeated, but still defiant, having held the Germans for days, outnumbered and out-gunned. Despite continued attacks during the day the perimeter stays largely intact. Increasingly, XXX Corps artillery is blunting German attacks. If only you had had this support a few days ago.

Nightfall brings your exit from the perimeter. It is very dark, with an inky sky, strong wind and heavy rain. Men drag themselves up from sodden ditches and begin to move south. Nearer the river the men hold hands or one another's smocks not to get lost. You leave in single file, making for the river bank and await your time for evacuation.

Eventually you are called over to a storm boat and make your way across the churning waters of the river. Even then you cannot rest; dawn is coming and there are still men under your command trapped on the northern bank. Over 10,000 of you dropped and just 2,163 will have returned.

110

It is not long before Hackett begins to come under pressure again. It is incredible how the Germans are so resilient. Despite the arrival of the Poles they have become as bold as ever and are attempting to push through the landing zone and threaten your northern flank. You desperately need news from XXX Corps.

By evening you receive the heartening news that they are barely five miles from the Arnhem Bridge. German resistance in the south is crumbling. You take the decision to withdraw from the landing zone and consolidate around Arnhem and await the arrival of XXX Corps. Now turn to **Decision 139**.

111

1530 hours 17 September 1944

News is still scant. But more groups of German prisoners are arriving and it is becoming clear that Lathbury is attempting to support Frost's thrust along the Lower Rhine southern road. However Lathbury's two other battalions have come across stiffening resistance in Oosterbeek. There is no news from the north, so you must assume that the units that landed there are progressing well in their allotted tasks. It worries you a great deal that you have no clear picture of what is happening. You presently learn that Gough has managed to link up with Frost. They set out much later than planned in the few jeeps they could scrape together. Gough's lead elements were also ambushed in thick woods to the east of Wolfhezen and have been involved in a running fight. Some of the prisoners now coming in are from Kraft's training battalion that had sprung the trap. Now go to **Decision 156**.

112

You stamp on the accelerator. The jeep's wheels spin on the cobbles. Glancing around you see the turret of the armoured car trying to track you and get off a shot. The Germans are too late; you round a slight bend in the road and disappear from sight. It was a close-run thing. Now go to **Decision 2**.

113

Your 600 or 700 men are evenly distributed to cover the southern and northern approaches to the bridge. You are stretched very thinly but so far the Germans seem to be unaware of your capture of the bridge. At around 0300 hours you decide to try to grab a few minutes sleep. You have barely drifted off on the sofa of one of the houses on the northern side of the river when you hear gunfire and explosions.

'A German column sir!' shouts a paratrooper as you head for the balcony.

You have a grandstand view of the slaughter below. There are half a dozen German trucks packed with unsuspecting German soldiers, caught in a cross-fire between your units on the southern side and blocked by more on the north. The bloody engagement is over in a matter of minutes.

'They know we're here now', you mutter and decide to try and get back to sleep for a while. Now turn to **Decision 15**.

114

Directly below you a German self-propelled gun has stopped. Some of the crew are making routine checks and others are chatting with soldiers, seven or eight yards away.

'Here goes', you whisper, pulling the pin out of a grenade and lobbing it through the open window.

The grenade drops right inside the vehicle. It rolls, bounces and then explodes. The flash sets off shell rounds and bullets. The crewmen have vanished, blown out of the vehicle and the other Germans are either lying beside the road or have run for their lives.

'Come on, no time to waste', you urge the other two.

Now turn to **Decision 199**.

115

'Get Hackett moving immediately', you order. 'Tell him to swing around to the north of Oosterbeek and cut off the German routes into Arnhem. Once he has done that he is to head south and link up with Lathbury and Frost.'

Now turn to **Decision 60**.

116

0600 hours 19 September 1944

You sense a real opportunity now, provided Hackett can successfully take the high ground to the north of Arnhem. Early reports are not good, however; all of Hackett's battalions are fully committed and he is making little headway. You learn that the northern flank of the drop zones are already in danger. You consider the options. If Hackett can push into Arnhem with all possible force, switching his line of attack to the south east, you will only have the Airlanding Brigade to protect the landing zones. If you want them to remain in position then go to **Decision 48**. If you want to shift the whole division to the east then go to **Decision 102**.

117

'We'll stay sir', Frost tells you. 'Make your way back to the division while you can. There's no point in your risking your life here.'

You know he's right. You need to try and coordinate the push towards the bridge. You have no idea what the progress is of the other battalions. Reluctantly you agree and you set off west, searching for advanced units. It takes you the best part of the rest of the day to work your way past German units, until you finally see paratroopers cautiously advancing ahead. Now turn to **Decision 32**.

118

You and Hackett decide to make a break for it. You steel yourself for the impending action. Your men break cover, with fixed bayonets. You charge forward; luckily few men are lost. You run on for half a mile and suddenly find yourself in the perimeter, on a stretch of the line covered by the Border Regiment. Breathless, you make for your HQ. Hackett sets up his own 50 yards away. Now turn to **Decision 137.**

119

0600 hours 21 September 1944

You send off a signal to XXX Corps and eagerly await a reply. It comes towards noon and makes promising reading.

'Irish Guards have pushed out of Nijmegen bridgehead. Have reached Oosterhout. Routes from Waal to Rhine on embankments bordered by marsh impassable to armour. ETA Arnhem earliest noon September 22.'

It may well be the time for bold action. If you want to launch an attack on the bridgehead to the south of the river using your existing units then go to **Decision 128.** If you think it would be advisable to drop the Poles on DZK then go to **Decision 9.**

120

From all reports the situation in the north is desperate. German units are infiltrating the perimeter and despite everything Hackett is being forced to give ground. To the east renewed attacks to dislodge you from the bridgehead have failed, yet there is no movement from the Germans from the south side of the river. It seems clear that XXX Corps is still moving forward and the Germans are too heavily engaged to launch a determined attack on the bridge. Now turn to **Decision 10.**

121

The medical orderlies are very busy; with unnerving accuracy German mortar bombs are landing around the crossroads. You hear the pained shouts of men hit by the mortar shells as they burst amongst the trees. Shortly afterwards Lathbury arrives. He is certain that the German troops are merely a local delaying force, but is as surprised as you are that they have recovered so quickly from the shock of your arrival and are fighting with such spirit and tenacity. Lathbury is concerned about the way the battle is developing.

He admits he is out of touch with the 1st Battalion and he presumes that it is moving along to the north of him. He has only intermittent contact with Frost's 2nd Battalion. You hear another mortar bomb strike nearby. It has hit your jeep and your signaller is badly wounded. Even now he is being evacuated by a stretcher party. The jeep is still operational but neither you nor Lathbury can raise anyone on the radio sets. Cursing the appalling communications you feel that the battle is slipping out of your control. If you think your place is back at the HQ then go to **Decision 71**. If you think that the battle is here then you should go to **Decision 83**. If you want to drive and try to link up with Frost then go to **Decision 97**.

122

In the darkness you can see the shapes of some paratroopers almost under the bridge supports.

'Who's that?' you demand.

'I think it's Major Digby Tatham-Warner. I've ordered a probe. It's already under way', Frost replies.

You can just make out small groups of paratroopers moving forward up the ramp. They get a few yards before coming under fire from a pillbox. The firing is supported by an armoured car that you can just see. It is sitting right on the bridge. The attack peters out and the paratroopers pull back. If you want to continue to wait go to **Decision 167**. If you wish to order a full-scale assault then you should go to **Decision 58**.

123

'There's nothing we can do', you say in resignation.

The German fires a warning burst through the window and you duck down to protect Lathbury. Taylor is hit in the arm. Three burly SS men barge into the room, barking orders and waving their machine pistols. You drop your automatic and stand up, your hands above your head. Your leadership of the opposition is now over and a period in a prisoner of war camp beckons.

124

0600 19 September 1944

Mackenzie sets off early to relay your message to Hackett. When he returns, he tells you that Hackett has all of his men committed and is desperately trying to push into Arnhem. He has detached a battalion to harass and hold the roads leading into the north of Arnhem, but they are under increasing pressure from German armour and infantry. Further news suggests that the intended drop zones for the Poles are under threat. Equally, the news from XXX Corps indicates that they are some thirty hours behind schedule, only having reached Grave. You know that should the Germans gain control of the Arnhem Bridge then they will be able to pour reinforcements south and hold XXX Corps. If you think it is best to let Hackett continue to push into Arnhem and attempt to turn the flank of the Germans opposing Lathbury then go to **Decision 61**. If you feel that Hackett's attack is futile and that he should withdraw and protect the drop zones then go to **Decision 17**.

125

'We're not going to make it in time', you tell your staff. 'I doubt Frost will be able to hang on to the northern approach for any more than a few more hours.'

The staff look disheartened and defeatism is beginning to percolate through the ranks. You know something has to be done, but without pressure from XXX Corps and dwindling supplies you doubt there is much hope. If you want to change your mind and press on with the eastern move then go to **Decision 171**. If you think you are right to call off the attacks then go to **Decision 91**.

126

0900 hours 20 September 1944

For the first time you appear to have reasonable news. Elements of the 2nd South Staffords have broken through to the bridgehead. Other battalions are passing you as they reinforce. By the end of the day the bulk of the division has quit Oosterbeek and is engaged in fighting in Arnhem itself. It has been at the cost of losing the landing zones. If you want to divert units to hold SDVZ, near Lichenbeek, go to **Decision 21**. If you think this is pointless then go to **Decision 162**.

127

You have barely run 10 yards when you are knocked to the ground. There is incredible pain and you cannot move. A medic does his best for you, but you can tell from the expression on his face that there is little hope. Perhaps you should not have been so willing to charge. Your command of the division is over, the mission a failure.

128

'We attempt an attack to take the southern approach tonight. We'll throw everything we have at it. 1 and 3 Para will lead, supported by the South Staffords and 11 Para', you inform your commanders.

Your men feverishly prepare for the assault. You know it is not going to be easy and that the Germans are fully expecting such an attack. As the afternoon passes you hear that the Germans have launched a major assault against your northern perimeter. Hackett is holding on as best he can, but he needs support. If you want to call off the attack and support Hackett then go to **Decision 80**. If you want to order Hackett to hold at all costs and go ahead with the assault then go to **Decision 68**.

129

1700 hours 21 September 1944

The original plan was for 1 Para Brigade to hold the southern side of the bridge and for the rest of the division, including the Polish Brigade, to hold Arnhem and Oosterbeek. Each day you deny the bridge to the Germans, the greater the chance for XXX Corps to break through. Nonetheless the Germans are mounting increasingly-violent attacks around your new perimeter. If you want to launch an attack on the bridge with your existing units go to **Decision 128**. If you feel that you need to coordinate with the Polish landings and have them drop at DZK then go to **Decision 9**.

130

Taking a track you head north, making for the main road again. The sound of gunfire in getting louder. Two more parties of German prisoners, with solitary guards, are on the road heading towards the landing zones. Suddenly you come upon the rear elements of the 3rd Battalion. A subaltern explains that Lathbury is closer to the front. You drive on and find the HQ set up at a major junction on the Arnhem-Utrecht road. On the corner of the junction is a Citroen staff car in Wehrmacht camouflage: the windows are shattered and the tyres flat. The door is hanging open and the body of the field commandant of Arnhem, Major General Cussin, is laying half-in and half-out of the car. Near the vehicles are the bodies of his batman and driver. You drive over to the Arnhem side of the junction and park the jeep under a line of trees. Now go to **Decision 121**.

131

You move into a large villa, set in a deep garden with immaculate lawns. You are made welcome by a tall, middle-aged Dutchman with greying hair. You apologise for the inconvenience but he replies that any sacrifice is worth getting rid of the Germans and in any case he is used to sleeping in the cellar because of the constant attacks by the RAF. You share a ground floor room with Lathbury, facing the road. In silence you eat some of your emergency rations, listening to sporadic firing outside. After eating you doze fitfully on a sofa, constantly alerted by the crunch of boots on gravel and half-heard conversations. You check several times to see if word has come from HQ, Gough or Frost. Before drifting off you and Lathbury send a signal to Frost, telling him that the rest of 1 Brigade would not make an attempt to reach the bridge until morning. The 3rd Battalion had clearly run into serious opposition and there were unconfirmed reports of seeing German tanks - older models but still potent. As darkness fell one of the companies had moved into a wood where it was engaged by German troops. In a nearby lane a PIAT had fired at a German armoured car scouting ahead. A few minutes later some five tanks and fifteen half-tracks had closed in behind the 1st Battalion. The last report came from Frost himself. He was at the bridge but urgently needed reinforcements. You decide that instead of the brigade trying to hold the high ground to the north of Arnhem an all-out effort would be made to reach the bridge. Now go to **Decision 98**.

132

You turn to one of the officers, an intelligence officer called Taylor, who is with Lathbury's HQ.

'We must try and get some proper medical attention for him.'

Taylor nods, but at that precise moment you spot a shape dodging around outside the window. If you wish to fire at the shape go to **Decision 142**. If you want to duck down and hide go to **Decision 3**.

133

0400 19 September 1944

Flashes of gunfire and shouting alert you to the fact that your troops are nearing the house. The self-propelled gun moves off, its tracks rattling along the cobbled street. A middle-aged Dutchman appears and excitedly explains that British troops are at the bottom of the road. Immediately you rush downstairs and make contact with a group of paratroopers, a mix of men from the South Staffords and the 11th Battalion. An officer tells you that HQ has been set up at the Hartstein Hotel in Oosterbeek. If you want to make for the HQ straight away go to **Decision 185**. If you wish to take a look at the progress yourself then turn to **Decision 47**.

134

0600 19 September 1944

Although you fear for Frost you know there is little you can do to help him. The operations map looks very concerning. Hackett is holding his own to the north of the drop zones. There are elements of 1, 3 and 11 Para on the outskirts of Arnhem. A single company of 3 Para has got through to Frost. Most of Arnhem seems to be under the control of the 9th SS. The most alarming news is that XXX Corps is thirty hours behind schedule. They have only just reached Grave Bridge. If the Germans manage to dislodge Frost from the bridge they will be able to send armour south, reducing the chances of XXX Corps ever getting to Arnhem. If you want to stick to your plan and hold then go to **Decision 17**. If you want to change the axis of your attack and try to break through with all your forces towards Arnhem then turn to **Decision 178**.

135

Frost offers to command the rearguard himself. You position yourself with Gough at the head of the break out. Your men manage to extricate themselves from the east side of the approach to the bridge. At first the Germans seem unaware of your intentions. Now go to **Decision 103**.

136

You spin the wheel to the right and slam hard down on the accelerator. The jeep squeals as it spins forward, a huge dust cloud billowing up behind you from the debris on the road. You see the Tiger tank edge forward, the commander barking orders at his crew. The hull machine-gun swings around to engage you. It is all very quick, very sudden and you feel nothing as the heavy machine gun rips into the jeep. You awake several hours later in a German hospital in Arnhem. There is no news of the fate of your division for days, as your war is over.

137

You try and make sense of the situation. Your battalions are very weak now and you desperately need reinforcements and supplies. Above all, you need to state how perilous the situation is now in and how imperative it is that XXX Corps gets here soon. You send off a signal, hoping it will get through: 'Enemy attacking main bridge in strength. Situation serious for 1 Para Brigade. Enemy also attacking position east of Heelsum and west from Arnhem. Situation serious but am forming close perimeter defence around Hartenstein with remainder of DIV. Relief essential both areas earliest possible. Still retain ferry crossing at Heveadorp.'

You make a last ditch attempt to get supplies through to Frost at dusk. Three Bren gun carriers attempt the breakthrough but two are lost and the third is forced to give up. Now turn to **Decision 198**.

138

You send off another signal: 'Intend to withdraw south. Feel it counter-productive to remain north of river given difficulties. Will collapse perimeter overnight and make for river south of Oosterbeek. Would be grateful for all assistance, particularly boats, DUKWs and rafts. Intend to complete evacuation before sunlight 24 September.'

You brief the officers and explain that your plan is for the best. A reply comes in while you are talking: 'Your pressure north still beneficial. However will leave you to decide whether DIV can hold for another 24 hours. XXX Corps confident of junction with you in Driel-Heveadorp area.'

If you would prefer to wait another 24 hours then go to **Decision 79**. If you think evacuation is imperative and needs to be carried out now then go to **Decision 93**.

139

1700 hours 21 September 1944

Hackett manages to disengage from his positions near the drop zone and consolidate himself in the northern outskirts of Arnhem. Casualties were surprisingly light. You receive a signal from XXX Corps as you are hastily eating an emergency ration pack.

'ETA half an hour Arnhem Bridge. Request demonstration from you to secure bridge. Put kettle on.'

It is fantastic news. Quickly you organise 2 Para to have the honour of meeting up with XXX Corps. it is the least you can do for Frost, whose stoic leadership has been an inspiration throughout the battle. At the last minute you decide to join him and his men as they cautiously advance across the bridge. Instinctively you all scatter and take cover as you hear tanks moving ahead. A Sherman tank comes into view, the tank commander waving furiously. Running alongside are British infantry herding hundreds of German prisoners. The commander salutes you and Frost then shouts: 'Got any room for this lot?' pointing at a line of dishevelled Germans. Next stop Berlin!

140

You drive along a winding, cobbled road. All of a sudden you involuntarily duck, as you speed along, reacting to a whizz and a ping as a sniper's bullet ricochets off the road surface close to the jeep. There is another shot, then another. Then you clear the gap in the buildings, doing 40mph. As you reach a row of shops you see your first bodies; a clutch of Germans and several paratroopers are down. Across the road a paratrooper gun crew has heaved a gun into a wrecked shop window. Others are running for the rear of the row of shops. A corporal steps out in front of your jeep, waving you down. Breathlessly he explains that a German armoured car is up ahead. He cautions you to stop and get off the road. You demand to know where Frost is, but the corporal shrugs and suggests he is ahead, somewhere closer to the railway bridge. If you want to take the corporal's advice then go to **Decision 166**. If you want to drive on and find Frost then go to **Decision 27**.

141

You watch with fascination as you see a pair of sappers creeping forward with a flamethrower. They manage to get into position and then fire up the weapon. The arc of the flame misses the pillbox and strikes one of the huts. There is a tremendous explosion, a blinding flash and the whole area is rocked. The huts are stacked with ammunition: tracer, small arms fire and mortar bombs accompany the explosion. You shield your eyes against the glare.

'I hope the bridge hasn't been lost', you wonder out loud.

'It looked sound enough. Now what?' asks Frost.

If you want to call off the assault then turn to **Decision 149**. If you want to go ahead then you should go to **Decision 85**.

142

You fire your automatic and the window shatters. The German is hit and he drops to the ground out of sight.

'Good shot sir," Taylor congratulates you.

The old Dutch couple that own the house try to explain that they will make sure Lathbury gets to the hospital across the road. You nod in agreement and pull Lathbury to a safer position under the stairs. You say your farewells and slip out of the back door. Now go to **Decision 46**.

143

You order a signal to be sent requesting that the Poles' drop zones are changed. The operations map makes sober reading. Hackett is just about holding his own to the north of the main drop zones. Scattered elements of 1, 3 and 11 Para are in the outskirts of Arnhem. Only a company of 3 Para has made it through to the bridge. It seems that the 9th SS have virtual control of the rest of Arnhem. You then receive the shattering news that the lead tanks of XXX Corps have only just reached Grave: this means that Horrocks is thirty hours behind schedule. It is even clearer now that if the Germans dislodge Frost from the bridge they will be able to pour reinforcements south to blunt XXX Corps' attempts at a break through. If you want to stick to your plan then go to **Decision 17**. If you want to change your axis of attack and try to take Arnhem with all your forces then go to **Decision 178**.

144

German half-tracks are following up the attack. These are easier targets for your men, who lob grenades into the open tops. Black smoke covers the whole area as burning fuel streaks across the road, engulfing the crippled vehicles. All momentum disappears from the German attack. It begins to disintegrate into a series of individual struggles. More vehicles burst into flames as the remaining German half-tracks and trucks find no escape. Two vehicles crash through the barrier of the bridge and plummet into the street below. SS troopers risk jumping into the Rhine rather than face your fire, or the flames burning their vehicles. The attack has been a catastrophic failure and over half of the German vehicles have been destroyed. Now turn to **Decision 195**.

145

1900 hours 20 September 1944

Hackett coordinates an attack on German units in the Lichtenbeek area and overruns the landing zone. Meanwhile, the KOSB pushes north east into Arnhem to affect a junction with Hackett's 10 and 156 Para. By nightfall 1, 3 and 11 Para have affected a complete link with Frost at the bridge. The

South Staffords and the Border Regiment are protecting the rear and have reached the outskirts of Arnhem. Hackett tells you that it may be practicable for the Poles to land at the supply zone after all. If you want to investigate this possibility then go to **Decision 94**. If you would prefer to hold them in reserve for a possible landing to support an attempt on the bridge then go to **Decision 154**.

146

'We'll take huge casualties doing it', argues one of your officers.

'I know that. Take the bridge in daylight, impossible', you agree. You send a terse signal back to Corps: 'Request impossible to follow. Will sustain unnecessary casualties.'

'Perhaps we should give it a go', Mackenzie suggests.

If you want to stick to your decision then go to **Decision 55**. If you want to change your mind go to **Decision 24**.

147

1530 hours 17 September 1944

The paratrooper salutes and grins as you pass. You cross the main road and turn right into a winding, narrow road that descends towards the river. So far you can see no signs of the fighting. But there is the ominous sound of gunfire coming from the direction of Oosterbeek. You notice just how undulating the terrain is around this part of Holland; very good defensive ground, particularly with the high wire fences that seem to surround many of the houses. Now go to **Decision 175**.

148

Slamming the jeep into reverse you back off as quickly as possible. Out of the corner of your eye you can see the turret of the armoured car tracking your progress. Suddenly you hear a crack then feel a shocking impact. Engulfed in flames, the jeep shudders to a halt. You are badly wounded. The signaller appears to be dead. In a futile gesture you rummage for a hand grenade as a second explosion rips the jeep apart. You can only hope that Lathbury can achieve your objectives, as your part in the operation ends here.

149

'Regroup!' you shout. 'This isn't going to work!'

You decide to wait until more men move up to reinforce Frost's battalion. There is little way of knowing when or if this might happen. With darkness having fallen it would be perilous to even try to get through to the other battalions around Oosterbeek. Flashes of gunfire and the occasional flare light up the sky. The bridge appears to be still intact. You shudder at the prospect of the Germans holding the south bank and barring the way of XXX Corps. If everything is going according to plan the British tanks should be here by the end of the next day. You fear that the longer you wait the greater the chance the Germans will have to establish a strong defensive line. Equally you worry about your rear. If the other battalions do not close up on your positions soon then the Germans are likely to slip strong units between you and them. If you want to launch a new assault on the bridge then go to **Decision 85**. If you would prefer to wait then go to **Decision 73**.

150

'Hold Hackett back for now. His original orders were to take the high ground to the north of Arnhem. We can't risk it now. We need to hold on to what we have. Lathbury will have to break through to Frost on his own for now', you order.

Now turn to **Decision 32**.

151

You hear an ominous sound; the clattering of tracks off to your right. All of a sudden an enormous Tiger tank emerges from the dust and rubble. It's hull machine gun rakes the ground ahead of your jeep as the turret begins to swing in your direction. You hear shouting to your left; German infantry, supported by a half-track. You need to act fast. If you want to drive forward then go to **Decision 172**. If you want to reverse go to **Decision 106**.

152

The rumours are correct, but there is little time for celebration. Throughout the day the Germans have been constantly pressurising you from the north and the west. There have been continued attacks from the east, toward what remains of Frost's command. At least you are beginning to be able to filter fresher units into the bridgehead. By the end of the day the bulk of your division is now in Arnhem. Oosterbeek has been largely abandoned. The landing zones are gone and you can expect little in the way of resupply. If you want to make sure that the SDZV supply zone near Lichenbeck remains open then go to **Decision 21**. If you think this is wasteful of your resources at this point then go to **Decision 162**.

153

'Charles, fancy getting your feet wet?' you begin. 'Make it clear to them Charles that we're terribly short of men, ammunition, food and medical supplies and that we need some DUKWs to ferry the Poles across. If the supplies don't come tonight it may be too late.'

You accompany him down to the riverside, going as far as you dare. You send Lieutenant Colonel Eddie Myers with him. Myers is from the Royal Engineer HQ and has hidden an inflatable dinghy that they are planning to use.

'Above all, do try and make them realise over there what a fix we're in', you tell him.

Now turn to **Decision 8**.

154

0600 hours 21 September 1944

'Request resupply on SDZV only. Priority anti-tank guns, PIATs and ammunition. Hold Polish Para Brigade in reserve. May consider move on southern bridge approach.'

You wait for several hours for the reply.

'Agreed. Expect supply drop before dusk today. Confirm hold on Polish drop. Suggest DZK at your discretion. Will wait for instructions.'

So far so good. If you can hold the landing zones for now your options will be greater. Now turn to **Decision 129**.

155

0600 hours 22 September 1944

Hackett's line has been pushed back so it is barely a mile from the bridge itself. You can hear the constant firing. With the bridge in your hands you can commit extra battalions to the north and immediately despatch the South Staffords and 11 Para to support him. A signal brings better news: 'Polish landings confirmed at DZK noon. XXX Corps at Elden to support landings.'

This is fantastic news. If you can hold for another few hours then the operation will be a complete success. Now turn to **Decision 41**.

156

Conflicting and inaccurate messages are still arriving at the HQ. Patiently you wait for concrete news, knowing that the primary objective of the Arnhem bridges must be your major concern. You know that the 2nd Battalion moved off for their six-mile march to reach the Arnhem bridges some time ago. Frost would have kept up a steady pace using the southern route, codenamed Lion, running from Heelsum via Heavadorp and Oosterbeek. Beyond Oosterbeek one of the companies would be detached to take the railway bridge. If you wish to remain at HQ then go to **Decision 44**. If you want to try and find Lathbury and Gough go to **Decision 13**. If you would prefer to find Frost and see if the bridges have already been captured then you should go to **Decision 57**.

157

A couple of minutes later you come across a pair of paratroopers hobbling back towards the landing zones. Both of them have been wounded. They look battered and bruised but still in good spirits. You apologise for not being able to take them to safety, but they tell you that Frost is just ahead, or at least he was half an hour ago. The railway bridge is down and he is moving his men to attack the road bridge. It is pretty good news and you decide that you need to be there to witness the assault. Now go to **Decision 14**.

158

You decide to commit the 2nd Battalion South Staffords into the push for the bridge to link up with Frost. For now it is all that you can do, but when Hackett's men arrive you are determined to push them into the battle to permanently seize the bridge. By then XXX Corps will be close, perhaps close enough to cooperate with you in a major attack to take both ends of the bridge. Now turn to **Decision 74**.

159

You are quickly updated on the situation. Hackett has landed and is trying to take the high ground to the north of Arnhem. Reports suggest he is running into serious opposition. Lathbury is pressing ahead toward Arnhem, but on a broad front and is making slow progress as German resistance is stiffening. Hackett's men appear to have bypassed Oosterbeek, threatening the German flank. His lead units are now in the outskirts of Arnhem, further south-east than planned. If you want to order Hackett to keep north and approach Arnhem from the north as planned then go to **Decision 124**. If you are content for him to act as he sees fit then go to **Decision 169**.

160

What remains of Gough's reconnaissance unit roars off south, heading towards Nijmegen. He has barely been gone for a quarter of an hour when you hear firing and artillery to the south. You know it won't be a particularly easy mission for him and you can only hope that XXX Corps is close. Now turn to **Decision 104**.

161

It is becoming clear that the Germans are throwing everything they can at your lines. Progress, if at all, is painfully slow. You hear from Gough that the situation is desperate. Now turn to **Decision 188**.

162

'Everything moves into Arnhem. We consolidate the bridgehead and if the opportunity arises we make an attempt on the southern approach. We can try and coordinate an attack with a Polish landing on DZK, near Elden on the south bank', you tell your assembled officers.

Now turn to **Decision 54**.

163

2100 hours 21 September 1944

The Germans launched attacks on Lonsdale's force in the southern part of the eastern side of the perimeter at 1840 hours. Then they struck the Border Regiment in the west just after 1900. The intention seems clear; to force you away from the river. The worst news is that the ferry crossing has been lost. On the far side the Poles, under Sosabowski, have managed to get as far as the river, but finding no boats or rafts, have been forced to take up defensive positions around Driel. It is a chilly and sullen night. You head out on your rounds to discover that your perimeter is 1,000 yards at the base, broadening to 1,200 yards and no more than 2,000 deep. You fire off another signal in desperation: 'No knowledge elements of DIV in Arnhem for 24 hours. Balance of DIV in very tight perimeter. Heavy mortaring and machine-gun fire followed by local attacks. Main nuisance SP guns. Our casualties heavy. Resources stretched to the utmost. Relief within 24 hours vital.'

You need to be sure that Corps are in no doubt about the situation. If you want to send Mackenzie, your main staff officer, across the river to make the situation plain then go to **Decision 153**. If you think the signal is sufficient then go to **Decision 8**.

164

0600 hours 25 September 1944

The evacuation of the wounded is achieved without a hitch. But no sooner has it been completed than the Germans renew their attacks. You have a tenuous hold on the perimeter and at 0800 hours German artillery and mortars begin pounding your positions again. A signal from Browning makes it clear that you should now withdraw across the river. You signal back, stating that you will attempt it tonight.

During the afternoon the Germans continue to infiltrate your perimeter. A group of Germans seize a wood barely 100 yards from your HQ. With incredible accuracy XXX Corps artillery bombards them out. If only you had had this support earlier. You burn all your papers and leave in single file, making for the river. As you reach the bank you see wounded men being loaded into the boats. You grimace as you hear the chugging of the storm boats. Eventually it is your turn. The boat seizes halfway across and drifts for a few minutes, but is restarted. Overhead you see the flashes of artillery fire as XXX Corps covers the evacuation. You reach the south bank, fearful for the men left behind. They are your gunners of the Light Regiment, firing their guns until the last minute.

The first grey light of dawn reveals your evacuation to the Germans. The last boats are gone. Some take the chance to swim. The operation is over at a cost of 1,200 officers and men.

165

'Alright, we'll shift emphasis and focus on the bridge. Call off the drop for now', you order your radio operator to signal.

The original plan was for 1 Para Brigade to hold the southern side of the bridge and for the rest of the division, including the Polish Brigade, to hold Arnhem and Oosterbeek. Each day you deny the bridge to the Germans, the greater the chance for XXX Corps to break through. Nonetheless the Germans are mounting increasingly violent attacks around your new perimeter. If you want to launch an attack on the bridge with your existing units go to **Decision 128**. If you feel that you need to coordinate with the Polish landings and have them drop at DZK then go to **Decision 9**.

166

Nodding assent, you reverse the jeep to the side of the row of shops and clamber out. No sooner have you done this than you hear a roaring engine and gunfire. Peering around the edge of the building you see the paratrooper anti-tank gun fire off a shot at a fast moving German armoured car. It misses by inches. The enemy vehicle begins to reverse, but a second shot slams into the side of it. Seconds later it erupts into flames and no one escapes the burning wreck. The paratroopers cheer and rush forward, scattering a handful of German infantry following up behind the armoured car.

'The road's a bit clearer now sir', reports the corporal.

You thank him and then climb back on board the jeep. It is still hazardous on the road, but you are determined to find Frost and discover whether the bridges have been captured. Now go to **Decision 2**.

167

You decide it is better to wait until first light. By then more reinforcements will have arrived and you will have a better chance of taking the bridge. In the darkness it is impossible to know what may be lying in wait for you. Taking a last glimpse at the objective, you are reasonably pleased that at least the northern approach is safely in British hands. On the bridge a couple of vehicles are burning. Every now and then there is an explosion as a box of ammunition or shells explode. If everything else is going according to plan then XXX Corps should reach you by the end of tomorrow. Now go to **Decision 149**.

168

Weapons poised you await the inevitable. The door flies inwards, shards of wood scatter across the floor. There is a burst of machine-pistol fire then three burly shapes crowd the remains of the doorway. Taylor is hit in the arm. The other officer, Cleminson, opens fire with his Sten, only to be shot in the chest. You drop to your knees and shoot the first German as he steps forward. Cursing, the other two Germans empty their magazines into you. Your leadership of the operation is over.

169

0600 19 September 1944

Sensing a real chance to turn the course of the battle, you send Mackenzie to order Hackett to push into Arnhem with all possible force. Your flank to the north worries you a great deal. Only the Airlanding Brigade is holding the perimeter of the drop zones. You wrestle with the options, knowing that you have insufficient forces to hold the drop zones and push through to Arnhem If you want to retain the Airlanding Brigade around the drop zones then go to **Decision 48**. If you want to shift the entire division east then go to **Decision 102**.

170

'We've got to hold them!' you scream, urging your men to resist.

A pair of 6pdrs sited in the open street turns the lead enemy tank into a flaming wreck. The other German vehicles try and work their way around the burning tank, only to expose themselves to more fire from your men. One by one you watch as the armoured cars and half-tracks are reduced to burning, twisted metal. The narrowness of the streets to the east and west of the ramp has done you a great service; the Germans simply lack the space to manoeuvre. This time you have been lucky, but you doubt the Germans will give up yet. Now turn to **Decision 62**.

171

'They're holding on', you tell your staff, 'we need to make every effort to break through to them. It's our only real hope. If the Germans take the bridge then any chances of XXX Corps getting here will be scuppered.'

At noon your decision seems to have paid off. The HQ is buzzing with rumours that lead elements of the 2nd South Staffords have managed to break through to the bridge. Other battalions are following up and you feel it is time to move HQ closer to the bridge. Your rear is still of concern, but you are slowly collapsing your defences in the west and moving them east. Now turn to **Decision 152**.

172

Slamming your foot down, you speed out of trouble, only to discover that your way is barred by another Tiger tank. The tank commander is holding his hand out to signal you to stop. He means to take you prisoner. If you want to obey him go to **Decision 6**. If you want to try and drive around the tank and escape to the east, as reversing is now impossible, go to **Decision 136**.

173

'Right, so we stay. Hicks you have three companies of the Border Regiment, the surviving KOSBs, the Independent Company, our Polish friends, the glider pilots and the sappers. Hackett the remainder of the 10th and 156th, the 1st Light Regiment and what remains of 1, 3 and 11 Para.'

The two officers murmur their agreement.

'So far the Germans haven't made a concerted attack on us, just scattered small-scale actions, but that might change. I've thought things through and will order that the Poles land at Driel on the other side of the river. They can reinforce us by getting across the ferry.'

Now turn to **Decision 163**.

174

As the sky fills with aircraft the Germans become bolder. It is a dangerous time but on this occasion a disastrous one for the Germans. Coming in waves to support the landings are hordes of allied fighters. Typhoons streak down on the German vehicles; other aircraft concentrate on shooting up the German infantry. It is over in a matter of minutes. The German thrusts around the drop zone are crushed. Burning vehicles litter the whole area. All that remains is to decide whether to hold the drop zone any longer now that the Poles have arrived and you have adequate anti-tank weapons. If you want to hold the zone go to **Decision 110**. If you think it now pointless go to **Decision 182**.

175

You soon come across the rear elements of Frost's 2nd Battalion. A sergeant tells you that Frost is with the leading companies, pushing towards the railway bridge. He explains that Gough's reconnaissance squadron was ambushed near Wolfhezen and was in a running battle with some SS troops. From what the sergeant understands Gough then got a message from you to make for Lathbury's HQ. It is clear from the sound of battle, the occasional crump of a mortar shell and the smoke up ahead, that the bulk of Frost's battalion is heavily engaged. You have to decide where you can do the most good and, above all, whether to take control of the battle. If you want to push on and link up with Frost then go to **Decision 140**. If you wish to make for Lathbury's brigade HQ then go to **Decision 130**.

176

0700 hours September 18 1944

The situation at dawn is still confused. Throughout the night the Germans have been trying to coordinate a series of attacks against your perimeter. You have already identified a number of German units, including a Panzergrenadier training and replacement battalion, and a number of obsolete tanks from the 6th Panzer Replacement Regiment. At dawn the main attack comes in with German troops trying to infiltrate your positions from the east. Suddenly the attack breaks off. There is an eerie silence that lasts for several minutes. You then hear the whine of shells, as the whole area is plastered with artillery and mortars.

'Here it comes!' you shout. 'Make ready!'

A German armoured reconnaissance unit bursts into view. It is a column of light tanks, armoured cars and half-tracks. They clatter under the bridge ramp and drive into Markt Straat. If you want to hold and fight back then go to **Decision 170**. If you feel you will be overwhelmed if you remain in position and wish to order a withdrawal you should turn to **Decision 18**.

177

'I think you made that choice just in the nick of time', announces Mackenzie, one of your staff officers.

'Why?' you ask.

'We've just had a report from Wolters, the Dutch liaison officer. He is in Arnhem now and got through to us via the telephone exchange.'

'Very resourceful of him: what's the report?' you reply.

'About sixty German tanks heading into Arnhem from the north. Seems to be that they came from the Deelen airfield.'

'Is he sure?' you demand.

'Pretty much. He said he would confirm the report as soon as he could.'

'Didn't we have unconfirmed intelligence that a Panzer Corps was refitting in the area?' you remember.

'Yes, but it was pretty vague', Mackenzie replies.

'Not so vague now is it?' you answer.

Now turn to **Decision 60**.

178

Belatedly, you decide that you need to focus all your forces on the push into Arnhem. You send Mackenzie off to order Hackett to press forward towards Arnhem. Early reports suggest that Hackett has encountered strong enemy formations and that his casualties are mounting. German resistance is strong. If you think it is futile to waste Hackett's men in such a manoeuvre then go to **Decision 17**. If you want him to press on regardless you should turn to **Decision 61**.

179

'Get them to dig in where they are', you order. 'We have to hold ground now, not throw our men at tanks.'

The situation is getting desperate; Hackett's men seem to be the only ones with any real strength left in the battalions. The rest of your command is being slowly bled away.

As night falls you ponder your options, which are becoming increasingly limited. Hackett has been engaged all day and cannot report in person as to his progress. You understand he is trying to push east and then south, but your intelligence is limited at the moment. If he has made any real headway then the Germans should be finding themselves under pressure, but there is no sign of it yet. Now turn to **Decision 90**.

180

Shortly afterwards you receive a communication from Gough. It is in code, just in case the Germans are listening to the phone call. He tells you that things are desperate at the bridge.

'I'm afraid you can only hope for relief from the south. For the moment we can only try to preserve what we have left', you tell him.

The Germans have tightened their hold on the perimeter around Frost's positions. Gough finishes the call by telling you, 'It's pretty grim; we'll do what we can.'

Now turn to **Decision 77**.

181

1200 hours 23 September 1944

Incredibly, the plan works to perfection. A sizeable German force near the ferry found themselves under intense fire from the south bank and then assailed by avenging paratroopers. Moments later 200 Poles landed on the north bank to complete the rout. Desperately your men begin to dig in around the ferry area. The Polish commander, Sosabowski, joins you shortly after nightfall, bringing with him the bulk of the rest of his brigade.

'130 Brigade is established south of the river. Now the decision has to be made as to whether we remain or evacuate,' he tells you.

However, the decision has already been made. A signal from Browning confirms: 'Roy, you are to evacuate the DIV immediately. Sosabowski will remain in place and be last to withdraw. Imperative you do this by first light.'

'That's it then?' you conclude.

Under cover of darkness the evacuation is a success. 2,500 men are withdrawn, a quarter of your original strength. Sosabowski's men manage to make it in the early hours of the morning. After a week out-gunned and outnumbered your men are safe. In your official report of the battle you write: 'The operation was not one hundred per cent successful and did not end quite as we intended. The losses were heavy but all ranks appreciate that the risks involved were reasonable. There is no doubt that all would willingly undertake another operation under similar conditions in the future. We have no regrets.'

182

You order Hackett to withdraw from the landing zones and take up positions in the northern outskirts of Arnhem. The Germans are quick to seize on the move and harry Hackett the whole time. You order your artillery to concentrate on the ground Hackett has surrendered. As you survey the new perimeter and consult with your commanders a breathless soldier rushes up to you.

'Sir, you've really got to see this. I mean the bridge', he tells you.

'What exactly?' you puzzle.

'XXX Corps. They're only here aren't they!'

Now turn to **Decision 200**.

183

Lights off, you begin your perilous journey through the deserted streets of Oosterbeek. You sense movement on the side roads and there are sounds of vehicles and tanks. It is too much to hope that they are British and you dare not stop and investigate. Twice you are challenged by German voices, but you simply flash your lights and drive on. The drive seems to last an eternity yet you keep on track, heading for the bridge. Now turn to **Decision 14**.

184

By mid-morning the main landing zone is well protected. The 7th KOSB, under Lieutenant Colonel Payton-Reid, are hard at work keeping the Germans at bay. It is their job to defend the landing zones.

At times the Lieutenant Colonel had to resort to age-old tactics; bayonet charges to force the Germans away. At around 1400 hours you can hear the steady drone of aircraft overhead. It is Hackett and the second lift. You watch in awe and horror as the situation unfolds. Air bursts hit several of the gliders and Dakotas. One aircraft with sixteen men aboard is hit and set alight. But you count as each of the men jump to safety. Another glider swerving off track, belly flops into some trees. It hangs amongst the branches, broken, with a jeep and anti-tank gun hanging from it. The whole heath is a mass of fire. You fear the worst, but in fact the landing is successful. 4 Parachute Brigade is largely intact, but you must decide where it can be best used. If you want to use it to secure the landing fields then go to **Decision 16**. If you want to use it to reinforce Lathbury then go to **Decision 177**.

185

Cleminson decides that he had better find 3rd Battalion, but Taylor accompanies you in the jeep. You take the lower road and as you approach a steep stretch you are exposed to German snipers from across the river. You tell Taylor to hold on tight as you put your foot down. You slam the accelerator and speed forward. You hear bullets pinging around you and it makes you feel like a target on a shooting range. Finally reaching HQ you are updated. Hackett, in the north, aiming to take the high ground, has run into strong resistance. Lathbury's units are still pressing towards Arnhem but have run into stiff opposition. You need to decide on your main objective now that the situation has entirely changed. If you wish to put all your effort into pushing towards Arnhem and linking up with Frost then turn to **Decision 4**. If you believe that it is imperative that the divisions stay together and hold on to what has been taken then go to **Decision 134**.

186

0600 hours 19 September 1944

You send Mackenzie off to order Hackett south east. Hackett has already anticipated your intentions and is threatening the flank of the Germans opposing Lathbury and the rear of those engaged in trying to dislodge Frost from the bridge. Hackett's casualties are mounting and German resistance is ferocious. If you think it is futile to fritter away Hackett's Brigade then go to **Decision 17**. If you want him to press on regardless of losses then go to **Decision 61**.

187

With a single anti-tank gun and some PIATs you are in a weak position to hold off the attack. A lucky shot strikes one of the German light tanks and it slews across a junction, blocking the road. The German vehicles stack up behind it, making easy targets for your men, who engage them at close quarters with PIATs, grenades and Bren guns. After a stiff fight the Germans begin to back off, blooded and in confusion. They head off the same way they came; it was a close run thing. Now turn to **Decision 191**.

188

0900 hours 20 September 1944

You manage to contact Hackett and he tells you that his whole brigade is engaged: 'We have a certain number of tanks among us', he tells you.

You need little imagination to picture the situation. From your current understanding, apart from 2 Para at the bridge the entire 1 Para Brigade has been virtually wiped out. The South Staffords have nearly ceased to exist as a unit and the 11th Battalion has fallen apart. The Germans seem to control every approach into Arnhem. If you want to still try to press forward then go to **Decision 180**. If you want to try and form a new perimeter on the northern side of the river, in the hope that XXX Corps can make it to you then go to **Decision 51**.

189

Your only major problem now is the landing zones that have been lost. Allied to this, you need to tell the RAF that you require resupply elsewhere; otherwise all of your drops will fall into German hands. Equally it is clear that the only remaining drop zone north of the river is vulnerable. This needs to be protected, but it is believed to be unsuitable for landing airborne troops. This fact rules out dropping the bulk of the Polish Parachute Brigade. Their intended drop zone to the south of the river, DZK, near Elden, is in German hands. A garbled message from XXX Corps indicates that they are struggling to take the Nijmegen Crossings. Now turn to **Decision 36**.

190

0600 hours 23 September 1944

It is grey, damp and misty, with a persistent drizzle. All around the perimeter the Germans are still using the small-unit tactics of clutches of infantry, supported by self-propelled guns, tanks and flamethrowers. By mid-morning the German attacks have ousted your men from positions to the east of your HQ. You are troubled by the threat that the Germans will cut you off from the river. You send another report: 'Spasmodic shelling and mortaring during the night, otherwise little change in the perimeter. Several attacks by infantry and SP guns or tanks supported by extremely heavy mortaring and shelling are in progress on north-east corner of perimeter. Fifty Poles ferried across river during night. Leading infantry 43 DIV have arrived on the south bank. Hope they will be able to cross under mist. Supply situation serious. Majority no rations last 24 hours. Ammunition short – latter may be accompanying party from south.'

Now turn to **Decision 39**.

191

'We can't possibly hold them off if they try that again', you state.

You are in no doubt at all that you need to concentrate your forces. If you want to pull everything back to the north side of the river then go to **Decision 62**. If you want to head for the south side of the river go to **Decision 75**.

192

Although perilous, you manage to find Hackett. He is with what remains of 156 Para. You greet him, but you can see that the battalion has been badly mauled.

'We don't know where the main German strength is. They seem to be everywhere', he tells you.

'I know. The situation is confused', you admit.

You strike out, heading south, but are soon confronted by smock–wearing soldiers standing in the open.

'Come on Tommy, come on!' one of them shouts.

'Could they be Poles?' Hackett suggests.

'Maybe', you answer.

If you want to go forward and talk to the men then go to **Decision 52**. If you would prefer to wait then go to **Decision 7**.

193

0600 hours 21 September 1944

The original plan was for 1 Para Brigade to hold the southern side of the bridge and for the rest of the division, including the Polish Brigade, to hold Arnhem and Oosterbeek. Each day you deny the bridge to the Germans, the greater the chance for XXX Corps to break through. Nonetheless the Germans are mounting increasingly violent attacks around your new perimeter. If you want to launch an attack on the bridge with your existing units go to **Decision 128**. If you feel that you need to coordinate with the Polish landings and have them drop at DZK then go to **Decision 9**.

194

You can see German troops moving into position. It is becoming clear that they intend to attack the hollow under cover of darkness. If you want to try and break out now before the Germans are in position then go to **Decision 118**. If you think it better to wait then go to **Decision 53**.

195

1800 hours 18 September 1944

Pressure continues to mount against your precarious hold on the northern approach to the bridge. Throughout the day the Germans have launched a series of uncoordinated attacks from Arnhem. It is now clear that the whole of the town is virtually in German hands and that the prospect of reinforcement from the rest of the division is unlikely. Equally, there is still no sign or word from XXX Corps. There are enormous numbers of British and German wounded in the cellars of the houses around the bridge. Ammunition is low and many of your men are now using German weapons. If you want to try and break out and head west with what remains of the force go to **Decision 19**. If you want to stay put then turn to **Decision 197**.

196

You gather together your officers and explain the plan. You propose to slowly withdraw the northern most units, have them pass through the other units then spearhead the small-scale attack on the ferry. You will abandon Hartenstein and re-establish HQ in or around the church to the south of Oosterbeek. Regrettably you must leave the majority of the badly wounded. What remains of 156 Para will be assigned the job of shepherding the walking wounded to the south.

'There it is gentlemen, Corps will support us as best they can. I'm hopeful that Polish troops will join us near the river for the attack on the ferry. Also I'm hopeful that additional support will be ferried over the river elsewhere.'

Hackett in particular seems sceptical about your plan. He feels that the perimeter is fairly secure for now and it would be foolhardy to abandon it. If you want to change your mind and call off the attack then go to **Decision 39**. If you want to press on with your plan go to **Decision 181**.

197

0600 hours 19 September 1944

The Germans have tightened the perimeter overnight. German Tiger tanks are creating havoc in the area. Your anti-tank gun ammunition is nearly gone and you are down to a handful of PIAT rounds. You speak to Gough whose men are holding part of the defence line nearest the river. You ask him about the situation.

'It's pretty grim. We'll do what we can', he tells you.

If you think the game is up, and think you should strike west to try and link up with the rest of the division then go to **Decision 76**. If you want to hold go to **Decision 5**.

198

0900 hours 21 September 1944

You have serious decisions to make, so you call a division conference. For the time being you divide the defence of the perimeter into two commands; Hackett will take the east and Hicks the west. You understand that you have around 3,000 men in the horseshoe-shaped perimeter area. Whilst you still have control over the ferry crossing at Heveadorp there is hope.

'The options gentlemen:' you begin, 'we retain the perimeter as long as we can. There is nothing we can do for Frost now I'm afraid. The primary mission has failed. Alternatively we begin to collapse the perimeter now and evacuate across the ferry.'

Ultimately you know it is your decision. If you want to retain the perimeter on the northern bank of the river go to **Decision 173**. If you want to start an evacuation then go to **Decision 92**.

199

No sooner have you emerged from the house than you come under fire from scattered groups of German soldiers. The whole place seems alive with them, a very disconcerting fact given that you were led to believe that the area was only thinly defended. The more you see the greater the doubt you have about the intelligence you were supplied with before the operation. You can either head west in the hope of linking up with Lathbury's lead elements and go to **Decision 100,** or you can try and break through to Frost by turning to **Decision 87**.

200

You leap into the jeep, taking Hackett and the paratrooper with you. You arrive just in time to see the first Sherman tank rumble down the northern ramp of the bridge. Behind it are more tanks, followed by half-tracks full of cheering British infantry. Behind them is a huge line of German prisoners being herded along by jubilant soldiers.

'Finally!' you shout, smiling and clapping Hackett on the back.

Frost appears at your side. Somehow he has managed to find a bottle of champagne. He pops the cork and you celebrate your victory. Perhaps the war will be over by Christmas after all, Monty was right!

Obergruppenführer und General der Waffen-SS Wilhelm Bittrich

It was as a former fighter pilot from the First World War that Bittrich began his involvement with the SS in 1932. By 1938 he had switched roles to become the commander of the second battalion of the Deutschland Regiment. For a short time, Bittrich commanded the Der Fuhrer Regiment, but on 1 June 1939 he moved to the Liebstandarte to work as Sepp Dietrich's HQ Adjutant. After the Polish campaign in 1939, Bittrich's promotion was rapid.

On 14 December 1940 he became Regimentskommandeur of Deutschland and after Hausser, the commander of the 2nd SS was wounded, he took his place. Bittrich served as the divisional commander until January 1942. In May, he had to step down due to illness. Bittrich was assigned as the commander of the SS Kavallerie Brigade in May 1942.

In February 1943, he took command of the 9th SS Panzer Division 'Hohenstaufen', which was stationed in France until the spring of 1944. Due to the deteriorating situation in southern Russia, the division, along with the 10th SS Panzer Division, was sent to support the First Panzerarmee, which was in danger of being surrounded. The two SS divisions fought their way through an area of swamp to relieve First Panzerarmee and help extricate them.

Following this operation, the 9th was then sent to Tarnopol, which was also encircled by the Russians; this attack was only a partial success. The division then went into a general reserve for the Heeresgruppe Nordukraine until the middle of June 1944, when they were sent to France. It took the division nearly a week to get into position for their attack on the Normandy beachheads. In the event, their attack was called off due to a renewed British attempt to take Caen, which began on 26 June 1944.

Instead, the division was used to support the German line to the west of Caen. The engagement, lasting until early July, cost the division around

1,200 casualties. They were thrown back into the fighting on 8 July, with engagements being fought around Eterville, Maltot and Hill 112. The latter changed hands several times, with the 9th supporting the 10th.

On 10 July 1944 Bittrich assumed command of the II SS Panzerkorps. After 12 July the 9th was taken out of the line as part of plans to launch a new local offensive on 15 July. They fought a desperate battle for Hill 113 on 17 July, which was particularly ruinous for the Panzergrenadier battalions.

A major British push on 18 July broke the German line and the 9th was withdrawn for much needed reorganization. It was then sent east to operate as a reserve under the command of I SS Panzerkorps. By 25 July the division was ready again and was sent to the south of Caen to assist the 272nd Infantry Division whose lines had been compromised. They fought here for the remainder of the month, stabilizing the line as best they could.

On 1 August 1944 the 9th was rushed to Beny-Bocage to deal with a sudden crisis. They were now under the command of the II SS Panzerkorps. After a week of intense fighting the British thrust was blunted and they were able to be redeployed in the period 13–16 August to the Putanges area. The front line was breached again and the division was sent to the Vimoutiers region and was engaged on the northern side of the Falaise pocket at Merri and Trun. The 9th were able to keep the pocket open until 21 August 1944.

Shortly afterwards, the whole II SS Panzerkorps was withdrawn to refit. They retreated northwards through France into Belgium and then crossed the Dutch border. The 9th arrived in the Veluwe area to the north of Arnhem on 7 September. Three days later, the 9th received orders that they were to be transferred to Germany for a full refit. This meant they had to hand over many of their weapons and vehicles to the 10th SS: the latter division would remain in the Arnhem area to regroup. The 9th were actually on the verge of leaving for Germany by train when news of Allied airborne landings around Arnhem and Nijmegen took place.

Ultimately, the 9th would be tasked with defending the Waal Bridge at Nijmegen and blocking Allied attacks from the south, whilst the 10th was given the job of holding Arnhem itself.

During Operation Market Garden, SS-Obersturmbannführer Walter commanded the 9th SS Panzer Division 'Hohenstaufen'. Harzer was, in fact, the temporary commander, after the original commander SS-Oberführer Friedrich Wilhelm Bock had been wounded during the retreat from Normandy. Harzer was to prove himself to be a capable commander, able to react to changing situations on the battlefield.

The 10th SS Panzer Division 'Frundsberg' was commanded by SS-Brigadeführer Heinz Harmel. Harmel found himself in a more difficult position, as some of his units were trapped to the north of Arnhem and he had the unenviable job of trying to hold the line at Nijmegen.

At around 1315 hours at Vught (to the north of Eindhoven), Generaloberst Kurt Student stared up into the sky from the roof of his headquarters. He was watching a vast armada of Allied aircraft passing overhead. He then saw hundreds of paratroopers floating down to the east of his HQ. Student is reported as saying at the time:

'This mighty spectacle deeply impressed me. I thought with reflection and longing of our own airborne operations. If ever I'd had such means at my disposal. Just once to have this many planes!'

Student quickly realizes the purpose of the drops: the Allies intend to capture the bridges at Eindhoven, Grave, and Nijmegen. It makes sense, particularly as he is already aware that there are vast Allied forces building up to the south of the Maas-Scheldt Canal.

A quarter of an hour later at 1330 at Doetinchem (to the east of Arnhem) Bittrich receives a report that enemy airborne forces are landing at Arnhem. This is followed by confirmation that the Allies have in fact landed at both Arnhem and Nijmegen. His immediate reaction is that the operation aims to isolate the Fifteenth Army to allow the Allies to drive straight into Germany across the captured bridges.

Bittrich must order the 9th and 10th into action immediately. The priorities are to:

1. Attack the landing grounds to the west of Arnhem
2. To ensure that Arnhem and the bridge remain in German hands
3. Move to Nijmegen and prevent the Allies from seizing the crossings

Meanwhile, however, Arnhem has to be defended by SS Major Sepp Kraft and his 16th SS Panzer Grenadier Training and Reserve Battalion. They are encamped in woods near Wolfheze. Originally they had been in the Tafelberg Hotel in Oosterbeck, but this has been commandeered by Field Marshal

Model who has set up his headquarters in the hotel. Incredibly, Kraft can now see paratroopers landing just a few hundred yards from his new HQ. Kraft quickly realizes that the Arnhem Bridge is the main objective. His unit is the largest one anywhere near the landing zones at Arnhem. He needs to respond very quickly to the situation. One company is pushed forward to attack the landing zones, the second digs in to cover the two main routes into Arnhem, the railway and the Wageningen road. After a brief attack, the first company pulls back and rejoins the defensive company: they immediately attract a hail of Bren gun and rifle fire.

If you wish to take the role of Bittrich in the campaign, just turn the page and read **Decision 201**.

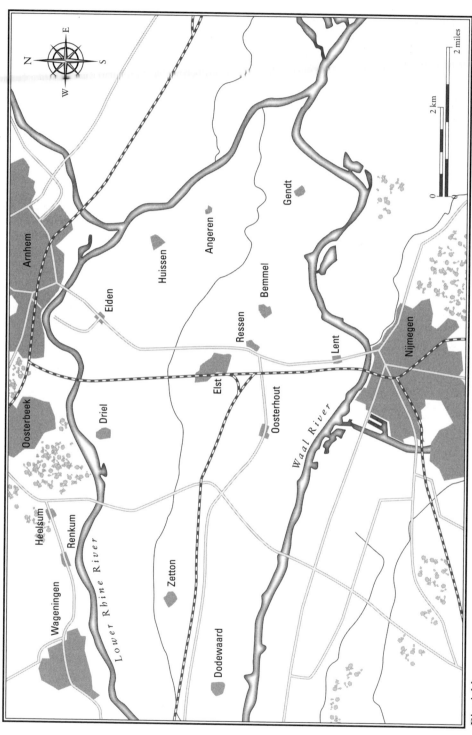

Bittrich's map.

Battleground General: Arnhem – German

1330 hours 17 September 1944

It takes you 10 minutes to quickly process the situation reports. Clearly the reports of enemy paratroopers have to be taken seriously. You signal the 9th SS Panzer Division and 10th SS Panzer Division headquarters and give them a warning order. You identify Arnhem and Nijmegen as the key objectives of the enemy. A plan begins to form in your mind; the 9th SS will carry out a reconnaissance of Arnhem and Nijmegen. The division will then assemble as quickly as possible and defeat the enemy landings at Arnhem and Oosterbeek. It is imperative that this is achieved with the minimum of delay. Meanwhile the 10th SS will assemble and head south, occupy Nijmegen Bridge and form a bridgehead to the south.

Several problems immediately rear their heads. Firstly Heinz Harmel, your commander of the 10th SS, is not yet back from Berlin. You sent him on a mission to lobby for more men and equipment for the corps. Secondly, your corps is dispersed and it will take time for it to assemble and move in force to the intended locations. This brings with it the danger of the enemy air force, perfectly capable, as you discovered in France, to wreck any attempts to move in daylight. No doubt, with an airborne operation such as this the enemy air forces will be out in force, hunting for likely targets.

To begin with your units react just like another staff command-and-control exercise. You hear that sizeable enemy forces have landed near both Arnhem and Nijmegen. Hazer, your commander of the 9th SS based at Beekbergen, receives your orders whilst he is at Hoenderloo. He orders his reconnaissance battalion, under Graebner, to prepare for a scouting mission to get better detailed information. His vehicles need work; the wily Hazer had Graebner partially dismantle them so they were not handed over to the 10th SS. He will need at least 2 hours. Nonetheless, by 1440 all of Hazer's quick reaction companies have been notified and declare themselves to be at 'action stations'.

If you want to confirm your orders at this time then go to **Decision 267**. If you want to wait for more information, turn to **Decision 292**.

202

1700 hours 17 September 1944

You drive on, finding SS Captain Moeller's command post. His limited force is fanned out along the side roads leading off Utrechtseweg, just to the east of Den Brink Park.

'Well?' you demand, striding up to Moeller.

'We're deadlocked in this jungle of gardens and mansions, the main road is a death zone.'

'What's the enemy strength?' you ask.

'There's no real front, sir, sections and half sections are fighting against similar-sized British units. There's no discernible line to the British side either', he replies.

You spot an abandoned train on the northern approach to the railway bridge and point in that direction.

'And that?' you demand.

'British bombers this morning. They damaged the embankment. Fighters strafed some Dutch workers that were trying to deal with it. SS Lieutenant Gropp's anti-aircraft Kampfgruppe is established near there.' he replies.

'We can't have the British take the railway bridge', you tell him.

If you want to order the destruction of the railway bridge then go to **Decision 373**. If you think this is unnecessary then go to **Decision 203**.

203

'There's no need to panic Moeller. We should preserve the bridge if possible', you say.

'Yes sir', replies Moeller. He does not look convinced.

You hear firing coming from the Oosterbeek area ahead of you. There must be more German units in the town. The situation remains perilous. You have identified that Moeller's men are fighting against companies of the British 2nd and 3rd Parachute Battalions. Moeller's battalion is awaiting orders. If you want them to advance then go to **Decision 316**. If you want them to remain in place then go to **Decision 374**.

204

A despatch rider screeches to a halt beside Henke. The rider seems puzzled for a moment, not knowing whether to report to you or to his own commander.

'The Americans have taken the Grave Bridge over the Maas. They're moving on the Heumen Bridge, over the Maas-Waal Canal. An entire division, believed to be the US 82nd Airborne', he tells you.

'That'll explain why they're not probing Nijmegen yet. Any sign of enemy movement in this direction?' you ask.

'Yes, sir. Reports of reconnaissance in force in the southern suburbs', replies the despatch rider.

So it appears that the US paratroopers are moving on the bridges. If you want to remain in defensive positions around the two bridges then go to **Decision 375**. If you want to order Graebner to probe forward and engage then go to **Decision 272**.

205

Graebner quickly informs you that he is engaged with lead elements of US airborne troops in the southern suburbs of Nijmegen. He doubts he can afford to disengage, as it will allow the enemy to move directly on Henke's scant forces that are defending the bridges. Now you are in a quandary. Arnhem Bridge is clearly under threat. If one side of the bridge is held by the enemy then the 10th must either force it from the north, or work their way around Arnhem and approach Nijmegen from a different direction. On the other hand, if you use Graebner now the threat to Nijmegen Bridge might be intensified. You can assume that the bulk of the 10th is backed up in Arnhem, waiting to get across the bridge. Either that or they have already left the town. You wonder if the 9th is strong enough to carry the bridge on their own.

If you want to insist that Graebner disengage and head north then go to **Decision 318**. If you want to rely on the forces that you have in Arnhem to take the bridge you should go to **Decision 206**.

206

'Very well, Graebner. Do what you can. Meanwhile I'll look at the options here. Break off when you can, as soon as the 10th SS or units further south can lend a hand. Is that understood?'

'Perfectly, sir', he replies.

Now turn to **Decision 376**.

207

'Moeller, order your men back', you shout.

'Too late, sir', Moeller yells back, ducking as a Bren gun opens fire.

'Fall back in sections!' you insist, making for a staff car.

You can see that already many of Moeller's men are either dead or are running. Disgusted, you snatch a fallen rifle and begin loading it. You fire off a few rounds as you pull away in the car. You realise that not only has the railway bridge been lost, but that the route through to the Arnhem road bridge is clear. Now turn to **Decision 299**.

208

'What's Harder's strength?' you ask Spindler.

'He's got three infantry companies and three operational Panther tanks I believe', Spindler tells you.

'Right. And he's closer to the bridge than Allworden?' you ask.

'Yes, but Allworden's strength is no greater, sir', Spindler replies.

If you want to send Harder towards the bridge then go to **Decision 338**. If you would prefer to wait, believing them to be of insufficient strength, you should go to **Decision 300**.

209

'Launch an attack now Harder. They can't be that strong here yet. We need to clear the bridge ramp and the approaches', you tell him.

Harder's small force begins to assemble, the sections each being briefed to focus on clearing their own part of the enemy defensive ring around the bridge ramp. You watch in silence, wondering if this is a mistake. If you wait there may still be some hope of artillery coming up. With artillery you could blast them out, or at the very least soften up the enemy positions and then launch a determined assault. On the other hand, the longer you wait the stronger the enemy might become, particularly if he can filter in fresh reinforcements. If you want to go ahead with the attack then turn to **Decision 381**. If you want to call it off go to **Decision 339**.

210

'Call off the assault before we have nothing left', you signal to Spindler.

Reluctantly he agrees with you. Graebner's men are now taking the brunt of the fire for the time being. You know how painfully exposed they are and that they can only come on virtually one after the next. Suddenly Graebner's force opens fire. The lead Pumas fire into the buildings around the northern ramp; for a moment it looks as if they are going to make it. Then the British open fire with PIATs, mortars and Bren guns; resistance is fierce from the enemy paratroopers. You see one Puma after another burst into flames. Still the firing goes on. Next in line for the punishing treatment are the half-tracks. The enemy throws in grenades to the open fighting compartments and shoots PIAT rounds. Black smoke boils up as blazing fuel engulfs the crews of the half-tracks. Graebner's attack begins to disintegrate. The SS troopers desperately seek refuse amongst the slaughter. Now turn to **Decision 379**.

211

The attack has obviously been a huge failure. Just one half-track reappears, carrying as many of the wounded as could be saved.

'You did your best, it was worth a try', you tell the men.

The troopers are dispirited, but still seem determined. There has to be other options to get the 10th SS to Nijmegen. It seems like someone has already been looking into this and you receive a signal that engineers have been sent to Pannerden to try and sort out the ferry. You decide to make for the ferry crossing to check the situation and see what options are available. As you reach there you see lead elements of the 10th SS Engineer Battalion. They signal you from the other side of the canal. You can already see that progress is going to be slow and it will be very difficult to get vehicles across the ferry.

Now turn to **Decision 254**.

212

0600 hours 18 September 1944

During the night you hear that the 10th SS has moved towards the ferry crossing at Pannerden. They hope that they will be able to cross here and then approach Nijmegen from the east, as you have ordered. You make the decision to look closely at the defences around Arnhem Bridge and to try to judge the strength of the enemy that has already dug in around those positions.

'Sir, there's armoured movement being reported on the other side of the bridge', Spindler tells you.

Terrible thoughts rush through your mind. It could be the enemy armoured column, but how could they have burst through and overwhelmed Eindhoven and Nijmegen so soon? With great trepidation you raise your binoculars and try to make out the vehicles. You stare for several seconds, trying to figure out what you are watching.

'I think its Graebner', you tell Spindler.

'You're right, he's going to try to rush the bridge!' Spindler replies.

If you want to launch an immediate attack on the northern side of the bridge to support him then go to **Decision 253**. If you prefer to leave the glory to him then go to **Decision 359**.

213

'Blow the bridge, Spindler, get the signal through to the engineers on the bridge!' you yell over the din of the battle.

'But sir, it can only be blown on express orders from Field Marshal Model', Spindler replies.

'I know that', you tell him.

If you want to insist that your order is carried out, go to **Decision 280**. If you want to call off the order you should go to **Decision 279**.

214

Four mortar rounds straddle the vehicle. The heavy tyres of the armoured car are shredded by the shrapnel. The driver struggles to control the vehicle, but it slams into a burning half-track. The impact is bone-jarring and you are thrown from the vehicle, exposed to the enemy fire. Another series of rounds explode around you, shattering your shoulder. You struggle to your feet and see Graebner's armoured car; it is wrecked and nobody has emerged from it. You stagger for a few metres, seeing an SS sergeant running to your aid. He never makes it; a Bren gun opens fire and cuts the pair of you down. Your command of the operation is over.

215

2400 hours 18 September 1944

Largely the news has been more promising today. The bulk of Reinhold's kampfgruppe has arrived and you have set up good defensive positions in Nijmegen, protecting the bridges. News to the south is less good. Apparently there are rumours that enemy tanks have been spotted heading towards Nijmegen from the south-west. If you want to check the situation for yourself then go to **Decision 283**. If you would prefer to wait until morning you should turn to **Decision 304**.

216

Slowing down, you reach the Grave Bridge. In the partial light you can see there is intense activity here. You suspect that it is elements of units tasked with cutting the corridor and that they are preparing to blow the bridge.

'General', your driver says, 'I don't think they are Germans.'

'Nonsense, they are either Dutch SS or Wehrmacht engineers', you tell him.

The car edges forward and suddenly an enormous bulk blocks your path. 'Get out of here!' you yell.

It is too late, however; khaki-clad men emerge from the shadows. They are British Infantry and the shape blocking your path is a Sherman tank. There is little point in trying to resist. Your command of the operations ends here and several years as a prisoner of war lay ahead of you.

217

This is an incredibly dangerous situation, which could threaten your whole defensive positions around Arnhem. To the south, elements of Von Tettau's forces are making steady progress along the Lower Rhine, but here, beyond the Ede-Arnhem railway, the whole area is in danger of being overrun. If you want to commit all men to beat off the new landings, you should go to **Decision 326**. If you feel it is better to fall back and hold the Arnhem perimeter area before it is too late, you should go to **Decision 391**.

218

'Harmel', you begin, talking on the radio, 'I need you to send a force to the south of Arnhem. Look for a possible landing zone.'

'Why sir, are there reports of enemy landings?' he asks.

'Not yet, but I suspect the enemy will attempt to take the bridge by the southern route', you explain.

Soon afterwards there is terrible news; US paratroopers and enemy armour have broken into Nijmegen. There are reports of vicious street fighting. You realise that without reinforcement nothing can stop the enemy from taking the bridges and Model will not allow their destruction. Now turn to **Decision 327**.

219

Kampfgruppe Knaust races towards the bridge approach as the enemy paratroopers continue to float down. They appear to be dropping further west, near Driel. It must be the Heveadorp ferry that they are after. News from the northern side of the river suggests that the British 1st Airborne is striking towards the ferry too. You wonder what they mean to do. This could either be reinforcement or an evacuation, but you cannot be sure. To the south an attempt by the British armoured column has failed to make much headway. Harmel has been forced to give ground near Bemmel, but the attacks on him have been somewhat limited. You order your men to wake you if anything happens during the night. But with mixed feelings you resolve to continue to resist in the morning. Perhaps firm news of the enemy landings at Driel will come through. Now turn to **Decision 263**.

220

0600 hours 22 September 1944

You continue to pressurize the enemy paratroopers to the north of the river. By 0730 hours there are still a great many of your men on the southern side of the bridge. Harmel has managed to evacuate his forces over the Pannerden Canal as ordered. The first air attacks begin just before 0800. Hordes of fighter-bombers strafe the bridge approach and cause chaos. You receive a report that a small British column is moving towards Driel. Rumours suggest that they are protecting a column of trucks with assault boats and amphibious vehicles. You need more intelligence to figure out exactly what they have in mind. You contact Field Marshal Model and bring him up to date with the situation. You know if he will not allow you to destroy the Arnhem Bridge then you might face catastrophic failure.

You decide to ask him: 'Absolutely not! If you don't have the stomach for a fight then I'm sure Harmel or Harzer will step into your shoes. Defend the bridge Bittrich. Destroy the enemy on the northern bank. We will prevail and strike back', he booms at you.

If you feel you have lost control of the situation and want to resign your command, go to **Decision 394**. If you wish to fight on then go to **Decision 242**.

221

0900 hours 23 September 1944

You receive reports that a handful of Polish paratroopers have been slipped across the Rhine during the night. Some supplies have also been sent over, but there is no sign of major activity. With the bulk of the enemy force in the south still failing to make any headway, you can feel optimistic at the moment. You head back to Doetinchem for a meeting with Field Marshal Model. He demands that you finish off the British airborne troops north of the Rhine within 24 hours. He needs the 9th SS to be deployed against the enemy in the south as soon as possible. If you want to go to Oosterbeek and consult with Harzer, go to **Decision 243**. If you want to head to Elst to check the situation on the southern front, go to **Decision 222**.

222

1900 hours 23 September 1944

Harmel assures you that the Nijmegen-to-Arnhem road can be held for another twenty-four hours. He has set up strong defensive positions all along the road, so the main road to Arnhem is untenable for the enemy at present. The problem is that he lacks the ability to block the road to Driel. Now turn to **Decision 266**.

223

0400 hours 25 September 1944

You are awoken with terrible news. Your commanders report that an entire division of enemy infantry has crossed the Rhine. Even now the 9th SS's positions are being shattered by artillery fire, and with impunity the enemy is building a Bailey bridge. Reports suggest long lines of enemy tanks and half-tracks massing on the southern bank of the river. Hesitancy has caused you to fail at the last hurdle. You know that your forces will not be able to hold them. Arnhem will be lost. Enemy armour will be across the river at first light. From the south there will also be an attempt to rush the bridge. You manage to contact Model and break the bad news to him. He is furious with your inactivity and blames you personally for the impending defeat. It is clear from the tone of his voice that your military career is over.

224

1500 hours 17 September 1944

You pause to think about the strengths and dispositions of your two divisions. The 10th is no more than a brigade in strength: some 3,000 men. There is a battalion at Deventer, another at Diepensen and a third at Rheden. There are some PzIVs at Vorden and artillery at Dieren; in effect a kampfgruppe. The 9th has also been reduced to brigade-strength. On paper they can muster some nineteen company-sized units, spread over twelve locations. The total strength stands at around 2,500 men. On average the units are 2 hours march away from Arnhem, or half an hour by truck if there are any available. Most of the units are billeted along the road running from Arnhem through Velp to Zutphen. Some are south of Apeldoorn. Although the bulk of the vehicles and heavy weapons have been passed over to the 10th, you realise that the 9th still has a reconnaissance battalion. Inexplicably Hazer reported that none of the vehicles were serviceable, but you suspect that he was simply trying to hang onto the vehicles for himself. You confirm the order to send the reconnaissance unit south to check out Nijmegen via Arnhem.

Shortly afterwards Field Marshal Model arrives. He broadly agrees with your decisions about the deployment of the two divisions. Together you work out the tasks and the coordinating instructions. Now turn to **Decision 313**.

225

The car is moving at around 20kmph, but you are more concerned about the damage to your uniform than bruises. You fling open the door and leap out onto the grassy verge; your dignity is more hurt than your body. The car continues for a few more metres, the sound of aircraft engines drones overhead. Suddenly there is a deafening din as the aircraft opens fire. The salvo riddles the staff car. The driver loses control and careers into a fence. As you stand up your driver emerges, shaken.

'Get down you fool!' you shout, hearing engines above.

Now turn to **Decision 247**.

226

'Graebner, continue towards southern Nijmegen as ordered', you shout.

He saluted and signals for the column to move on. Clouds of exhaust fumes swirl around the bridge's girders as the armoured column rumbles past. The camouflaged vehicles disappear from view. The scene falls silent and you can only hope that Ziebrecht, commander of the 1st Company of the 10th SS Reconnaissance Battalion arrives at Arnhem soon. His destination is Arnhem Bridge. To your attuned ears you sense that the battle is far closer than you expected. Suddenly you hear an enormous explosion. Even the bridge shakes.

'What the hell was that!' you yell, looking around for an explanation.

No one seems to have a clue. To the north-west smoke is curling up in an area around the Arnhem railway bridge. Someone has blown the bridge. The situation must be far more serious than you had imagined. If you want to remain here then go to **Decision 204**. If you want to head back towards Arnhem immediately then go to **Decision 335**.

227

The situation is quickly deteriorating. The enemy is closing on your positions. Despite the heavy fire Moeller's men are laying down it does not appear to have slowed the British advance. They are still pushing forward, taking possession of nearby buildings and raking your positions with fire. Any moment now Moeller's men will either break or the British will launch a determined charge on your positions. If you want to hold them, go to **Decision 273**. If you want to order a retreat, then go to **Decision 207**.

228

2400 hours 17 September 1944

It takes you some time to get to Pannerden. You discover that lead elements of the 10th SS Engineer Battalion have already arrived. They are trying to work out how to get the ferry ready for the tanks, half-tracks and other vehicles. You see that the progress is going to be slow. The engineers have begun their work in darkness and you know they will do everything possible to get the 10th across and into Nijmegen. Now turn to **Decision 254**.

229

What remains of Kraft's command appears to be falling back towards the northern outskirts of Oosterbeek. Spindler's men are establishing blocks on the Ede-Arnhem Road and trying to maintain some sort of contact with scattered units further south.

'What mobile units do we have Spindler?' you ask whilst staring at a map.

'Von Allworden's tank-destroyers and Kampfgruppe Harder', Spindler tells you.

If you want to order Allworden's troops forward then go to **Decision 274**. If you would prefer to focus on Harder's men you should turn to **Decision 208**.

230

2400 hours 17 September 1944

By the end of the day the news is very grim. Allworden made some progress but has been forced to withdraw in the face of heavy attacks from waves of British paratroopers. Meanwhile it appears that the British have slipped more men along the riverside. There are even some reports of British paratroopers forming up to attack the southern ramp of the road bridge at Arnhem. They must be using the railway bridge to slip across. All hope of being able to get the 10th SS across the bridge look to be dashed. This will mean that Henke and Nijmegen are on their own for now. Now turn to **Decision 301**.

231

'We throw everything we have at the bridge. If we can clear it we have a route straight through. Elsewhere we try to hold for now', you tell Spindler.

'There has been a signal from Graebner on the southern side of the river. He is going to try and take the bridge by storm', Spindler tells you.

'Excellent! We need to help him', you say.

Now turn to **Decision 253**.

232

'Break off the attacks, hold firm and turn to face the river. Support Graebner with fire if you possibly can', you order.

You stand in horror as the situation begins to deteriorate. The enemy is flooding the area with fire. Spindler's units nearest the river are disintegrating and your lack of support for Graebner has blunted his ability to break through. You can see the enemy picking off his vehicles one by one. If you want to order an immediate withdrawal, go to **Decision 323**. If you want to continue to fight, turn to **Decision 279**.

233

Harder's men have little hope. You spot Spindler and head back to him. He has set up a new command post only 20m away. Sporadic attempts to counter-attack by your SS troopers have ended in disaster, as the enemy gets bolder and bolder. Now turn to **Decision 384**.

234

You stand beside Graebner in his converted British Humber armoured car. The bridge begins to vibrate as you approach. The tracks and wheels are screeching on the surface of the ramp. The column surges forward as Graebner shouts through his radio set for his drivers to make maximum speed. The SS troopers hunch down for protection in the open half-tracks, in anticipation of the fire they will draw. Ahead a Puma armoured car disappears over the summit of the bridge and fires off its main gun and machine guns. Two more armoured cars surge forward, followed by three more. Suddenly you hear an explosion, as one of the armoured cars hits a British mine. Your vehicle clatters over the summit of the bridge and comes under concentrated fire from machine guns and mortars. As you close with the northern ramp grenades are tossed in your direction. Two half-tracks overtake you and immediately draw the fire. A grenade lands inside one of the compartments; the carnage is unbelievable. Vehicles are coming to a halt as their drivers are killed. This leaves the occupants dangerously exposed to fire from every angle. If you want to order Graebner to halt the vehicle before you get too close, go to **Decision 385**. If you want to press on go to

Decision 214.

235

'Hold here Euling! Wait until Reinhold gets here in force. Where is he?' you demand.

'He's crossing at Pannerden as we speak', Euling replies.

Euling's command is part of Reinhold's kampfgruppe and with that in place you can hold the defensive perimeter to the south of the bridge.

'News of attacks from the east against Groesbeek?' you ask.

'Corps Feldt is launching attacks, sir, but they lack the punch and I fear they will not make any real difference', Henke replies.

You suspect he is right. If you think you have done all you can here and wish to head for Arnhem now then go to **Decision 344**. If you think you should remain here you should turn to **Decision 258**.

236

'Get me Field Marshal Model', you order. 'Pull everything back across the river.'

It takes several minutes to establish contact with the field marshal but eventually you hear his voice. You quickly explain the situation to him.

'No. I will not permit it!' he tells you. 'We will prevail. The Fifteenth Army is poised to counter-attack. Hold firm Bittrich!'

Now turn to **Decision 305**.

237

'Very well, Field Marshal, I'll do what is necessary here', you concede.

At precisely 1300 hours the enemy artillery and tanks begin firing on your positions. They are joined in the attack by rocket-firing Typhoons. They swarm overhead, striking the area and smashing every vehicle or entrenchment they spot. Then you notice small boats on the water. Enemy soldiers are paddling furiously and heading for the northern bank. You stare in horror as they begin to cross, despite their casualties. Then they land. Your forward positions are overwhelmed. Another wave of enemy troops is making for the northern end of the railway bridge. The situation is now desperate.

'General, I urge you to reconsider!' you shout to Model over the radio.

'No! I forbid it!' he tells you.

'But Field Marshal British tanks are crossing!' you yell.

'Very well, do it', he finally concedes.

Quickly you give the order, but nothing happens. You scream the order again, but there is nothing. The charges must either be defective or the lines to them broken. If you think you should remain here and try and hold them back you should go to **Decision 259**. If you want to retreat you should go to **Decision 345**.

238

'You don't leave me with very many options Bittrich', Model begins. 'I'm relieving you of your command. Clearly you cannot see the bigger picture. If you think destroying the bridges is the only solution, when they actually represent our best chance to strike back, then you are not the commander I believed you to be. Harmel will assume command of the Corps. You are to report to Berlin, pending court martial.'

You try to protest, but he will not listen to you. Your command of the Corps is over.

239

0400 hours 19 September 1944

At least four battalions of enemy paratroopers are trying to fight their way to Arnhem Bridge. The hasty defence line has been established but it is weak and you suspect that the enemy will break through in the morning. Harzer is still trying to prize the enemy from their positions around the northern ramp, but resistance is fierce. By the afternoon the situation is worsening. There is also news that Nijmegen is on the verge of collapse and it seems that the bridges are in immediate peril. If you want to try and hold out for longer and leave Harzer to break the resistance at the bridge you should turn to **Decision 392**. If you want to pull back again and throw everything you have at the bridge to try and save Nijmegen, go to **Decision 261**.

240

You maintain radio contact with Harmel as his troops advance on Bemmel. The terrain is not ideally suited to fast movement, with just one road capable of coping with heavy traffic. So far, apart from some heavy artillery fire, the enemy has barely responded to this move. By 1100 hours Harmel's lead elements have reached Ressen. You then receive a report from him that the enemy armoured column is moving forward from the Nijmegen bridgehead under cover of hordes of Typhoon fighter-bombers. If you want him to continue with his manoeuvre then go to **Decision 348**. If you want him to switch around and form a defensive perimeter, promising him that you will send reinforcements to hold the rest of the line to his west, go to **Decision 287**.

241

'Ridiculous! Our positions are intact. Who knows what they mean by landing at Driel!' you shout.

You resolve to firm up your defences and the bridgehead and hold Harmel back as a precaution against a continued enemy thrust from the south. Just after noon a report suggests that the enemy is on the move. Harmel already knows and is racing to deny the enemy Bemmel and one of the key junctions. He reports that he is under heavy artillery fire and that the whole area is swarming with Typhoon fighter-bombers. Terrible thoughts of Falaise come back to you. You can order Harmel to continue his advance and promise to send help to re-establish a line that blocks the enemy advance to the south. If so, go to **Decision 289**. Alternatively, you can withdraw across the Arnhem Bridge and tell Harmel only to press on with the attack if the enemy moves forward and go to **Decision 368**.

242

0830 hours 22 September 1944

Reports suggest that the enemy has begun to advance along the Nijmegen-to-Arnhem road. Better news suggests that some enemy units have had to be diverted to counter-attack against thrusts organized by Model near Veghel.

The enemy thrust towards Arnhem will be weakened, which is excellent news. On the northern side of the bridge the enemy paratroopers have fallen back towards the Lower Rhine. Arnhem is no longer threatened from this direction. You can begin to reduce this troublesome pocket once and for all. Now turn to **Decision 369**.

243

1700 hours 23 September 1944

You order that all efforts must now be made to cut off the enemy airborne troops north of the river from the river itself. This will ensure that they are separated from the enemy on the opposite bank and cannot be reinforced or resupplied. Their only alternative will be surrender. If you want to head to Elst then go to **Decision 222**. If you want to return to your headquarters go to **Decision 266**.

244

0600 hours 25 September 1944

Slowly but surely the pocket is being squeezed. By 1400 hours your 9th SS has broken through in several places. The enemy is still resisting, but in ever-decreasing numbers. Upwards of 1,500 prisoners have already been taken, and most of them are wounded. At 1800 hours the final force of enemy paratroopers fight their way to the river bank and, under cover of fire from artillery, attempt an evacuation. You estimate that fewer than 500 managed to make it across. It has been a Pyrrhic victory. The 9th SS is shattered as a fighting force. You doubt they can be thrown back into action for months. The loss of Nijmegen and the ground between the town and the Rhine is catastrophic. The cost of retaking it will be ruinous. Germany must continue to resist, but the odds are not in your favour.

245

1600 hours 17 September 1944

It is a beautiful Sunday, with wonderful sunshine and also the promise of being a peaceful and uneventful autumn day. As you approach Arnhem you are astonished to see the wealthy homes, with their neatly laid out gardens. Even the little tracks have cobbles or tarmac. There are bicycle tracks running alongside the road and your driver, as a precautionary measure, veers off the main road and continues along the bicycle track as it gives you better cover from the air. Suddenly you hear a roaring sound overhead. Craning your neck out of the open window you stare up and see a number of twin-engine bombers overhead.

'Something is up', your driver begins, 'now we're for it'.

He could be right. If you want to order him to drive on then go to **Decision 268**. If you want to stop and pull under a tree to wait for the aircraft to pass then go to **Decision 293**.

246

'Take evasive action, keep moving', you order.

The driver, a man you have known for several years, is clearly scared. But he is devoted and instantly obeys, speeding up and zigzagging to present a poorer target for the marauding aircraft. The whole area seems to shake and the engine noise is getting louder. The staff car judders as several shells smack into it. The first volley shatters the windscreen and cripples the engine. Before you can move a second attack comes in; this time the heavy shells penetrate the car's roof. You feel intense pain in your back and left shoulder. Seconds later you pass out. Your part in the defence of Arnhem and Nijmegen is over.

247

Another series of thuds threaten to burst your eardrums as more explosive shells hit the car and roadway. Miraculously your driver makes it to the edge of the road, flattening himself with his hands over his head. You duck as a second volley of fire rips into the staff car. You know you need to get out of here and yell to signal a motorcycle combination to come and get you. You clamber aboard. It is not exactly the transport of choice for an SS general, but you roar off towards Arnhem Bridge. You pause under the awning of a shop as another enemy aircraft passes overhead. Now turn to **Decision 352**.

248

'Get a signal to the engineers, I want that bridge blown', you order.

'Yes, sir', replies Moeller, ordering two men to sprint to the railway bridge and alert the engineers.

Another immediate danger presents itself. The firing is getting closer. You need to hold the enemy back long enough to ensure that the bridge is destroyed. If you want to order Moeller's men forward to block the enemy's approach to the bridge then go to **Decision 249**. If you want him to establish a line here and hold them off, go to **Decision 317**.

249

Moments later you are nearly flattened by an enormous explosion. The railway bridge has been blown. It was just in time, as the enemy paratroopers could not have been more than 50m from the bridge.

'Now get forward. Here's our chance to stop them!' you urge Moeller.

Now turn to **Decision 319**.

250

You ride with the unit towards the ramp. For a time, as you rattle across the bridge, it appears that you are going to make it. Suddenly all hell breaks loose. Enemy anti-tank weapons and Bren guns open up on you. There are several near-misses, but it will only be a matter of time. If you want to press on go to **Decision 360**. If you want to call off the attack then go to **Decision 278**.

251

The firing is intensifying if anything. The British paratroopers are pushing forward. They are laying down very heavy fire on what remains of your positions. Even more worrying is the fact that enemy paratroopers in increasing numbers are slipping either side of your positions. There is an immediate danger of being overwhelmed or surrounded. If you want to order a withdrawal you should go to **Decision 357**. If you wish to remain in position for now then you should turn to **Decision 273**.

252

0600 hours 18 September 1944

The new day brings no better news. Your forces are backing up in Arnhem. The 10th has shifted to the Pannerden ferry and is trying to cross over into the ground beneath Arnhem and Nijmegen. Only in this way can they fulfil their mission to reinforce Nijmegen. There is a clear and stark choice now for the troops in Arnhem; you can either throw them at the Arnhem bridgehead established by the enemy, or you can attempt to hold back the rest of the enemy force still trying to burst through to Arnhem from Oosterbeek. From your understanding the German troops to the west of the enemy landing zones have made little progress. You can only expect more enemy reinforcements today. If you want to focus your attacks on the Arnhem Bridge then go to **Decision 231**. If you think it more prudent to focus on holding the line you should turn to **Decision 321**.

253

'Spindler, get your men prepared, launch an immediate attack. We need to press them now and help Graebner as much as we can', you order.

Spindler begins organising his troops as Graebner's armoured reconnaissance unit revs up and begins to cross the road bridge. You are sure you can see Graebner jabbing his fist to urge his men forward. He is riding in a captured British Humber armoured car. From here you can hear the tracks of his column rattling and screeching on the surface of the bridge.

'Come on Graebner!' you shout.

Spindler's men are moving forward, coming under heavy fire from the enemy paratroopers. There seems to be a lot of them. The interlocking fields of fire are cutting swathes into Spindler's forces. You can see the men hesitating as they expose themselves to the full wrath of the enemy's fire. If you want to press on with the attack then go to **Decision 277**. If you want to call it off then go to **Decision 210**.

254

0900 hours 18 September 1944

Attacks from the north, towards the enemy-held northern ramp, have failed. But the 9th has effectively cut off the British from reinforcement. An attack by Graebner from the south has also ended in failure. Graebner is dead and his unit has been badly mauled. This leaves options limited for now. It is impossible to take the bridge until more reinforcements arrive. If you feel you are better served at Nijmegen then go to **Decision 343**. If you think you had better be in Arnhem then go to **Decision 303**.

255

'Sir, I think there's movement, armoured vehicles, on the other side of the river', Spindler tells you.

'Quick, there's no time to lose', you tell him, clambering into a staff car and heading for the bridge area.

There is carnage everywhere. Clearly an attack by Brinkmann's 10th SS unit has ended in failure. There are knocked-out light tanks, armoured cars and half-tracks littering the area. There is black smoke belching from dozens of fires.

'It's Graebner sir', Spindler tells you, handing his binoculars over to you. 'He's making an attack on the south ramp.'

If you want to support Graebner's attack you should go to **Decision 253**. If you think he can handle it alone you should go to **Decision 359**.

256

'Graebner, good luck', you tell him, dismounting from the vehicle.

He returns your salute and smiles. The vehicles are revved mercilessly and then surge forward, led by a clutch of armoured cars. Graebner punches the air then extends his arm and the whole column moves forward. At first everything seems to be going according to plan. But then you hear mortars, machine guns and PIAT rounds firing off. You hear brakes squealing, yells and there is flame and smoke. The attack has clearly failed; catastrophically so. Your view is poor, even more so now it is wreathed in smoke and flames. You shake your head in disbelief and sorrow. Now turn to **Decision 281**.

257

'I want to establish a line of defensive outposts on the two traffic circles south of the bridges. We can reinforce as more troops arrive. Is that clear?' you tell Euling.

'Absolutely', he replies, saluting you.

'Henke, defend the approaches to the railway bridge. If Reinhold gets here today he will protect the road bridge', you order.

Reinhold's kampfgruppe, you understand, of which Euling is a part, is crossing by way of the ferry at Pannerden. They should be with you very soon. You are beginning to feel a little more confident about the defence of the bridges. This is assuming of course that the US paratroopers do not make a determined attempt on the bridge before you are ready. This factor concerns you a great deal. If you want to find out what is going on to the south-east then go to **Decision 386**. If you are content to wait then you should turn to **Decision 215**.

258

2400 hours 18 September 1944

You sleep in one of the houses in Elst, awaiting news. Reports filter in all night. Firm news arrives at 0820 when you hear that Grave Bridge has been reached by the enemy thrust from the south. All attempts by units trying to cut the airborne corridor have ended in abject failure. By midday you learn that only a Panzer brigade, the 107th, stands between the enemy and Nijmegen. However, you later learn that they are positioned far further south than you were first led to believe and will be no use to you for Nijmegen. Now turn to **Decision 387**.

259

1400 hours 20 September 1944

Your defences are collapsing and you see three or four self-propelled guns dug in near the bridges get knocked out in succession. You make for a pair of 88mm anti-tank guns. They are the only thing you have left to deny the enemy. Even this position is under threat, with American paratroopers rampaging towards you and a large column of British tanks bearing down on the positions. You know there is nothing to prevent the enemy from getting to Arnhem now. If you want to abandon the gun positions and retreat, go to **Decision 345**. If you want to remain here then go to **Decision 285**.

260

Ahead is a small copse, which your driver approaches with extreme caution. You stare out of the car window, trying to spot the men he said were hiding here. Suddenly a man steps out in front of the car. His uniform is unmistakeable. He points his rifle at the car. Your driver lunges for his pistol, sitting in its pouch beside the driver's seat. The soldier, without even blinking, shoots him dead. The man is a British paratrooper and now more appear at the side of the car.

'Look here sergeant, we've bagged ourselves a real German general', one of the men shouts.

Whatever the outcome of the struggle for the bridges, your command of the operation is over.

261

'Pull everything into Arnhem. Crush the bridgehead. Leave small units to hold up the enemy advance from the west', you order your officers.

It takes time, but shortly before nightfall the men are in position. But there are reports that the enemy to the west has advanced into the outskirts of Arnhem and is harrying your stay-behind units. Under a barrage of artillery and mortar fire your men and tanks grind forward to reduce the pocket and the bridge. It is a hard and dirty battle; no quarter asked or given. You are shocked by the casualties and the number of badly-wounded men on both sides being evacuated from the area. After three hours of terrible fighting, the last remnants of the British paratroopers surrender. The bridge is yours at last, but at a terrible cost. The 9th SS is shattered and the bulk of Arnhem is occupied by the enemy. Mobile units are sent south over the bridge. What remain dig in to hold the bridgehead. All roads in the north are now held by the enemy and it is you that is now cut off. If you want to remain here and hold the bridge, go to **Decision 328**. If you think it prudent to make for the south and link up with the rest of your corps then go to **Decision 288**.

262

0700 hours 20 September 1944

A new day brings fresh hope. Although your men are exhausted, it is clear that the level of fire and resistance from the enemy at the bridge is slackening. You order the attack to continue house by house, slowly reducing the enemy perimeter. At 1100 hours you receive a call from Field Marshal Model. He tells you that the 15th Army is attacking enemy paratroopers to the south of Nijmegen. The plan is to reinforce the town, and even take bridges further south back from the enemy. You are still concerned about Nijmegen and ask for permission to blow the bridges if they are threatened.

'We will prevail within the week, Bittrich. You will not destroy the Nijmegen bridges. Is that clear?' he tells you.

You speak with Harmel next and he tells you that the terrain between Nijmegen and Arnhem has only one road that can support tanks. If he could only have some artillery in place the enemy, even if they take Nijmegen, would have no chance of breaking through to Arnhem.

At 1300 you receive alarming news that the enemy is launching a determined attack on Nijmegen. Henke tells you the handful of the 10th SS that have made it to the town are insufficient to hold the enemy off. The signal from Henke is abruptly cut and you pace around your command post, waiting for communication to be re-established with him. Now turn to **Decision 393**.

263

0530 hours 22 September 1944

The situation is becoming clearer. Reconnaissance elements of the enemy armoured column have broken through your lines at Oosterhout, to the west of the bridgehead beyond Nijmegen. With reports confirmed that enemy paratroopers that landed yesterday have struck toward Heveadorp, the enemy plan is becoming more obvious. Your own immediate plans are clear; slowly give ground where necessary to the south, but to keep the line intact. There is only one major roadway to worry about that runs direct to Arnhem. Secondly, to continue to press the enemy at Oosterbeek to ensure that no option other than surrender or evacuation is possible for them. By 0830 hours it is clear that your southern line is still holding. Attempts by the enemy to push forward in force have stalled. If you want to check the situation at Driel, go to **Decision 330**. If you want to make for Elst and see how the line is holding up, go to **Decision 265**.

264

1200 hours 23 September 1944

As you head west through Arnhem and into the outskirts of Oosterbeek the signs of battle are obvious. The buildings are battle-scarred, wrecked vehicles litter the road and there are many dead. You need to head north now to avoid the front lines. But as you drive west and then south again you catch sight of the Lower Rhine. It is a mass of activity. Huge groups of amphibious craft are crossing the river. The area is shrouded in smoke and there is intense fighting. It seems obvious to you that the enemy intends to force the Lower Rhine. They can only hope to put Bailey bridges across once the northern bank is secure. This could explain why the enemy is pushing more infantry across the river. If you want to launch an all out attack on the Oosterbeek bridgehead, go to **Decision 290**. If you feel your forces are not adequate to do this then go to **Decision 310**.

265

1600 hours 22 September 1944

The line has had to give ground, but it is still firm. You wonder why, with all the armour and resources the enemy has, it has not punched straight through your thin line. You sense that the enemy will attempt a major assault soon. This places you in a difficult situation. You need to decide whether to hold the line as best you can in the south, or to order it to pull back over the Arnhem Bridge. You fear that when the attack does come your men will be overrun and trapped on the south side of the Rhine and slaughtered. If you want to continue to hold the line in the south, go to **Decision 311**. If you think you should order a withdrawal before it is too late you should go to **Decision 370**.

266

1700 hours 24 September 1944

After allowing a two-hour ceasefire on the northern bank of the river to allow the evacuation of British and German wounded, the fighting starts up again. You are perplexed, as the request for the temporary truce was made by a British doctor and not the senior commander, who you now understand is Urquhart. You wonder what lies behind this. Your suspicions are that Urquhart knows he is beaten and that the British intend to evacuate him, rather than reinforce him. If you want to call on Urquhart to surrender, go to **Decision 371**. If you want to order continued attacks through the night, go to **Decision 312**.

267

Rapidly you dictate your warning order and tell your staff to pass this on to the two divisions by telephone:

'Enemy: enemy air landings: main point of effort identified around Arnhem and Nijmegen.

Tasks:
9SS Pz Div – division is to recce Arnhem and Nijmegen – division is to assemble immediately, take Arnhem and defeat the enemy air landings by Oosterbeek west of Arnhem – absolute speed is necessary. The Arnhem Bridge is to be occupied by strong security forces.

10SS Pz Div – division is to assemble, move to Nijmegen and fully occupy the main bridge and to defend the Nijmegen bridgehead.'

Now turn to **Decision 224**.

268

'Drive, get amongst the buildings up ahead, they haven't spotted us', you order the driver.

Ahead the motorcycles are scattering. They have spotted something you haven't seen as yet.

'Fighter bombers!' the driver shouts, as a pair of the aircraft peel off and begin to dive in your direction. 'Get out sir, run for your life, I'll draw their fire.'

You need to react quickly. If you want to dive out of the moving car then go to **Decision 225**. If you want to order the driver to continue and zigzag then go to **Decision 246**.

269

1800 hours 17 September 1944

SS Captain Viktor Graebner's reconnaissance battalion comes into view. He has a column of thirty half-tracks and armoured cars. It is reassuring to see him. Only yesterday Graebner was awarded the Knight's Cross. He has 400 men, a powerful and mobile unit. If you want Graebner to continue on his mission towards the south of Nijmegen then go to **Decision 226**. If you think it is prudent to have him remain here until more troops arrive then go to **Decision 270**.

270

'Graebner, remain here. Deploy a defensive ring around the bridges. Coordinate with Henke and pull in any stragglers. Await the arrival of the 10th. Once they are here you are to hold the road between here and Arnhem. Is that understood?'

Graebner nods and dismounts. He begins barking orders at his men. At least the Nijmegen bridges are safe. All of a sudden there is an enormous explosion to the north-west. You stare in disbelief as part of the Arnhem railway bridge goes up in smoke.

'Who ordered that?' you demand

The situation must be far more serious than you had imagined. If you want to remain here then go to **Decision 204**. If you want to head back to Arnhem with all possible speed then go to **Decision 335**.

271

The firing has got progressively heavier over the past few minutes; regardless of Moeller's fire power the enemy is clearly closing. You can see the lead elements and a company peeling off and making for the railway bridge. You realise that the situation may already be lost. If you want to continue to hold the enemy back then go to **Decision 273**. If you want to order a withdrawal, go to **Decision 207**.

272

'Graebner, probe forward aggressively. Prevent the enemy from penetrating the town at all costs', you order over the radio.

For now there is little else you can do here at Nijmegen and you decide that the best option is to head for Arnhem and get a better idea of the current situation there. Now turn to **Decision 335**.

273

As the casualties mount Moeller's fire begins to diminish. The enemy is getting bolder by the second it seems. Now they are barely 50m from your positions. You can see pockets of the enemy slipping around your flanks. In seconds the engagement will be over. Moeller is desperately trying to urge his men to hold. Suddenly you are floored by a stunning impact in your chest. You crumple to the ground, bleeding heavily. The scene begins to fade but you can see German soldiers running either side of you. Six days later you wake up in a hospital bed. You discover that you are in fact in Antwerp and that you are under guard as a prisoner of war. At first no one will give you any news, or even talk to you. But after a few more days a British intelligence officer arrives to interrogate you. He tells you that the allied operation was a complete success and that they have crossed the Rhine in force. Now you know that the war has been lost. You are positive of it.

274

'Send Allworden west to block the enemy trying to bypass us by the northern route', you tell Spindler.

Allworden has enough men for three companies of infantry. They also have a pair of self-propelled guns and some 75mm anti-tank guns.

'Get them to attack the landing zones if possible', you tell him.

If you want to remain and wait for news you should turn to **Decision 230**. If you want to get a clearer look at the situation at the bridge then go to **Decision 320**.

275

'Signal Kraft and Gropp to fall back. There's little point in getting overrun. We're all that stands between the British and the bridge', you say to Moeller.

'It is probably too late already', Moeller replies, pointing at a steady stream of enemy paratroopers flooding past your positions nearest the river.

He could be right. All your blocking force has managed to achieve is to temporarily hold up the British advance in this part of the front. Elsewhere there is nothing to stop them. Now turn to **Decision 276**.

276

The withdrawal begins according to plan. As soon as the British spot that you are pulling back they renew their attacks with increased ferocity. Moeller tries his best to keep cohesion, but his men are few and exhausted. You dread to think about the rest of the front or what they are facing now they have abandoned their positions. If you want to leave Moeller to it and save yourself then go to **Decision 212**. If you want to remain with him then go to **Decision 273**.

277

Spindler's men are taking heavy losses as they fight their way forward. Graebner's men are under intense fire from the British paratroopers around the bridge. Something has to give. The volume of fire is reaching a crescendo as you see several of Graebner's Puma armoured cars sprint across the bridge and begin engaging the British paratrooper positions in the tall houses around the bridge ramp. This encourages Spindler's troops forward, making another last ditch attempt to link up with him. Still the enemy resists. There is hand-to-hand fighting around the bridge ramp and inside the houses. The ferocity of the combat is reminiscent of the worst that you have ever experienced. Little by little the enemy is giving ground. Suddenly you hear a roar and look to your left, towards the river bank, on the northern side of the river.

A huge new tide of enemy paratroopers have emerged and they are falling on the flanks and rear of Spindler's men. If you want him to turn and face the new threat then go to **Decision 232**. If you want to press on and establish a link up with Graebner then go to **Decision 322**.

278

'Pull back, turn around: we're dead if we continue', you shout.

A sergeant beside you signals to the others and abruptly they stop and begin to turn, constantly under fire. It is a difficult manoeuvre with so little space on the bridge. Miraculously you manage to get out of the situation, but it was a very close call. Generals should not really be getting this closely involved in actions. You determine to try to avoid situations like this again. There has to be other options to get the 10th SS to Nijmegen. It seems like someone has already been looking into this and you receive a signal that engineers have been sent to Pannerden to try and sort out the ferry. You decide to make for the ferry crossing to check the situation and see what options are available. As you reach there you see lead elements of the 10th SS Engineer Battalion. They signal you from the other side of the canal. You can already see that progress is going to be slow and it will be very difficult to get vehicles across the ferry.

Now turn to **Decision 254**.

279

'Hold them Spindler', you yell.

But already the situation is almost lost. With Graebner's threat blunted the British paratroopers already in position around the bridge are adding their fire, as your men try to get into new positions to hold off the enemy attack. Caught in a crossfire Spindler's men are being cut down. Any moment now the situation will be out of control. If you want to fight on then go to **Decision 342**. If you want to order a withdrawal you should go to **Decision 323**.

280

'Just blow the bridge, I'll take full responsibility', you yell back at him.

Spindler grabs the radio set and tries to contact the engineers.

'No contact, sir. The lines must be broken', he tells you.

There is nothing for it now. You can either continue to resist and go to **Decision 342**. Or you can order Spindler to fall back and go to **Decision 323**.

281

There has to be another option, another way to wrestle the bridge from the enemy. Besides which, the 10th SS needs to get to Nijmegen to hold off the enemy thrusts from the south. You desperately need information. If you want to make for Nijmegen then turn to **Decision 343**. If you want to try and work your way around to the east and get into Arnhem, go to **Decision 303**.

282

1400 hours 18 September 1944

Von Tettau has been attacking all day from the west and Harzer's men from the east.

'The enemy is dug in, sir. I suspect that we can expect enemy reinforcements to arrive soon', Harzer tells you.

'I suspect you are right', you reply.

As if to confirm your conversation you hear the noise first and then the sky seems to darken as literally hundreds of transports, bombers and gliders fill the sky.

'They're going to land on the heath!' you shout.

German fire concentrates on the vast armada, but although the situation on the ground descends into chaos, the bulk of the enemy force manages to land in strong groups all around the heath. A Dutch SS battalion, led by SS Captain Helle, is caught unaware. Most of his company flees in seconds. If you want to personally organise the effort against the unwelcome newcomers you should go to **Decision 217**. If you think Harzer is capable and you wish instead to link up with von Tettau to consult you should go to **Decision 390**.

283

Under escort you tentatively head south through the outskirts of a surprisingly-quiet Nijmegen. The railway is to your left, as you head towards Grave. It is deadly quiet and you continue for some kilometres before you can see lights ahead, near the Maas River. This is where the bridge at Grave crosses. You begin to seriously doubt whether the rumours are true about the progress that has been made by the enemy armour. If you want to turn back now then go to **Decision 304**. If you want to drive on towards Grave you should now turn to **Decision 216**.

284

1300 hours 20 September 1944

The enemy artillery and tanks begin firing on your positions. They are joined in the attack by rocket-firing Typhoons. They swarm overhead, striking the area and smashing every vehicle or entrenchment they spot. Then you notice small boats on the water. Enemy soldiers are paddling furiously and heading for the northern bank. You stare in horror as they begin to cross, despite their casualties. Then they land. Your forward positions are overwhelmed. Another wave of enemy troops is making for the northern end of the railway bridge. The situation is now desperate.

'General, I urge you to reconsider!' you shout to Model over the radio.

'No! I forbid it!' he tells you.

'But Field Marshal, British tanks are crossing!' you yell.

'Very well, do it', he finally concedes.

Quickly you give the order, but nothing happens. You scream the order again, but there is nothing. The charges must either be defective or the lines to them broken. If you think you should remain here and try and hold them back you should go to **Decision 259**. If you want to retreat you should go to **Decision 345**.

285

You manage to hold them off for another few minutes, but the sheer weight of numbers overwhelms your last positions. Reluctantly you raise your hands and surrender alongside your exhausted gun crews. Your command of the Corps is over. You can only hope that Harmel and the rest of the corps manage to block the enemy from getting to Arnhem. Your future is that of a prisoner of war.

286

0600 hours 21 September 1944

You instruct Harmel to launch a counter-attack at first light. He has managed to amass three or four kampfgruppes, supported by sixteen Panzer IVs. Your intention is for him to attack the enemy front lines that are slowly pushing forward from Lent. His attack will come from the west. His artillery support is weak and it will be firing from the east bank of the Pannerden Canal. Some of his units have not yet crossed the canal. You can only hope that Harmel's men can push far enough forward to link up with Knaust at Elst and form a cohesive line. His attack goes in as scheduled, but soon you realise that the punch you were hoping for is being cancelled out by enemy artillery positioned around Nijmegen. Harmel's forces are taking a terrible pounding. If you want to order him to continue and push forward to threaten Bemmel and Lent then go to **Decision 287**. If you want him to pull back out of range of the enemy artillery you should go to **Decision 347**.

287

1600 hours 21 September 1944

The move by Harmel has paid off. Knaust's kampfgruppe is firmly holding Elst. Panzergrenadier 21 occupies the line from Elst to Bemmel, and SS Panzergrenadier 22 is covering Bemmel itself. Here and there a few tanks from the 10th SS Panzer Regiment strengthen the line. From your position near Elst you hear the ominous roar of aircraft overhead. It is nearly 1700. Squadrons of British Spitfires appear out of the clouds. They circle around your positions in the Driel area. Suddenly they swoop down and begin to attack anything that they have spotted. Your men return fire in an attempt to protect themselves. Then there is the sound of other aircraft. You look up and spot enemy transport aircraft; Dakotas. They are flying very low.

It is another enemy paratrooper landing and already you can see countless parachutes in the sky. You quickly realise the purpose of the landings; they intend to use the Rhine ferry at Heveadorp. The ferry is not in German hands. The only other alternative you can think of is that they aim to seize the road bridge at Arnhem and cut off the 10th. If you want to despatch units to Arnhem Bridge to forestall this you should go to **Decision 219**. If you think that your line is compromised, go to **Decision 308**.

288

1800 hours 20 September 1944

Harried by enemy paratroopers closing in on you, you begin to collapse your tenuous hold on the perimeter. Dispirited, the men trudge across the bridge to the south, constantly under fire from enemy mortars. It is a perilous retreat, but one you feel is necessary. The bridge is still intact and perhaps you can regain it once you have reorganised your corps. As your last men leave the bridgehead you can hear the enemy cheering as they occupy your positions. Reaching Elst, you use the radio to inform Field Marshal Model of the disaster:

'This compounds everything! You've lost Nijmegen and now Arnhem!' he bellows.

'Nijmegen is lost?'

'Yes, about four hours ago, both bridges taken.'

'I take full responsibility for the failure of my corps.'

'Yes you will! And I would advise you to take responsibility even further and avoid the need for a court martial,' he says as he cuts the connection.

289

You fire off a flurry of orders to your commanders. Knaust and the bulk of Harzer's reserves race south through Elden, Elst and Ressen.

'Get to Bemmel. Establish the line there', you tell Harmel.

By the end of the day you realise that you have made this decision in the nick of time. The British armoured column has failed to make much headway. Harmel has been forced to give ground near Bemmel, but the attacks on him have been somewhat limited. You order your men to wake you if anything happens during the night. But with mixed feelings you resolve to continue to resist in the morning. Perhaps firm news of the enemy landings at Driel will come through. Now turn to **Decision 263**.

290

0930 hours 24 September 1944

Some progress has been made overnight, but the casualties have been extremely high. A British doctor, called Warrack, has asked for a temporary truce to evacuate the wounded. You can sense this could be the end, or at least the beginning of the end. You agree to the truce and promise that there will be a two-hour ceasefire at 1500 hours today. The firing recommences at 1700 hours. You are still unsure about the enemy's intentions. You cannot understand why they have allowed 500 of their wounded to become prisoners of war. You can see that your men have inflicted heavy damage on the assault boats deployed by the enemy, but if the rumours are correct a number of enemy troops have crossed over to the northern side of the river, although not nearly enough to make a difference. If you want to make another major attempt to attack the British on the northern bank, go to **Decision 350**. If you want to continue to press, go to **Decision 395**.

291

1600 hours 25 September 1944

Your troops continue to pressure the perimeter. But the weight of artillery support breaks up any serious attempts to cut the enemy off from the river. You are running out of time. Model demands results. He needs the 9th SS to be able to throw them into the defensive positions to the south. If you want to order an all out attack to overwhelm the perimeter today, go to **Decision 398**. If you feel that continued pressure is sufficient under the circumstances then go to **Decision 331**.

292

1500 hours 17 September 1944

Field Marshal Model arrives from his headquarters at Terborg. Model has the reputation of being a trouble-shooter. He has steady nerves and is an ideal man for a crisis. On several occasions his prompt action on the Eastern Front stabilised what had seemed to be lost causes. Above all, Model understands his soldiers, but he is a private, reserved man, with a strong belief in the Führer. Quickly, you outline the plans you have been toying with, the 9th to deal with the British at Arnhem and Oosterbeek and the 10th to race south to take and occupy the Nijmegen Bridge and secure a bridgehead to the south of the River Waal.

'Above all we cannot allow a link between the enemy forces around Nijmegen and those in Arnhem', Model tells you.

Together you draft an order to be telephoned to the two divisions at 1730:

'IISS Pz Corps is to immediately attack and destroy the enemy. The following forces are to be employed:

Within the boundaries of Arnhem Kampfgruppe 9SS Pz Div against Oosterbeek and the enemy bridgehead north of the Rhine. In Nijmegen Kampfgruppe 10SS Pz Div.

Now turn to **Decision 313**.

293

A pair of the aircraft drops down to investigate. It is clear that they have spotted movement along the road. A pair of motorcyclists has roared up the road to try and fool the aircraft. One of the enemy aircraft peels off and strafes the roadway, sending bursts of heavy machine-gun fire, kicking up the dirt and spraying the area. One of the motorcyclists is hit, another spins out of control and tumbles headlong into the road. The aircraft roars overhead, hunting for prey. You have not been able to rely on the Luftwaffe for months and this is just another case of the enemy having clear skies. The din of the engines finally recedes. If you want to move off then go to **Decision 294**. If you want to wait a little longer, turn to **Decision 352**.

294

'Drive on carefully', you order.

The driver puts the car into gear and pulls off. Seconds later you hear the drone of aircraft overhead once again. The enemy is hunting for targets and must have spotted you.

'They're fighter bombers', the driver tells you, as one of them swoops and opens fire on the motorcyclists.

Nervously you look ahead; there is no cover for at least another 500 metres. 'Jump out sir!' yells the driver.

If you want to get out of the moving vehicle then go to **Decision 225**. If you want to stay inside and zigzag to present a more difficult target then go to **Decision 246**.

295

You can only hope that Henke has matters under control at Nijmegen. You know he will only have a scratch force available to him. You pass through the outskirts of Elst, heading south. You cross the railway, and then for a second time as you approach Nijmegen. Now turn to **Decision 314**.

296

'Deploy your men, Moeller. We have to hold here', you order.

Moeller begins shouting orders at his scratch-sections. Quickly they set up firing positions covering the main road. Horrified you watch as a huge enemy force comes into view. They are moving forward at a jog. A company detaches itself and makes for the railway bridge. The bulk of the force continues in your direction. Quickly you realise that not only is the bridge in immediate danger, but you are at risk of being instantly overwhelmed. If you want to remain in position and assist Moeller then go to **Decision 297**. If you think it prudent to get out of the area immediately then go to **Decision 354**.

297

The firing starts as the enemy begins to close. Despite the casualties the British paratroopers press on, closing with your position. In moments the situation begins to look even more dangerous than you could have imagined. There seem to be hundreds of British paratroopers, oblivious of the fire, pressing forward, probing in strength, occupying houses and laying down a withering fire. You quickly realise that there is every chance that they will simply overwhelm you. If they do then nothing lies between them and the bridge. If you want to hold them, go to **Decision 273**. If you want to order an immediate withdrawal, go to **Decision 207**.

298

0600 hours 18 September 1944

It takes until morning before Graebner is in a position to rejoin you. The fighting has been inconclusive, his casualties slight so far.

'I want you to attempt to force the Arnhem Bridge', you tell him.

'Understood', he replies.

'Intelligence suggests that the northern ramp is held by the enemy. We need to clear the bridge to get the 10th SS across and into Arnhem', you explain.

If you want to join him on his mission you should go to **Decision 380**. If you think you are better served by heading for Pannerden, where you understand the 10th SS intends to use the ferry crossing to get to Nijmegen, go to **Decision 361**.

299

1830 hours 17 September 1944

The situation is desperate. Nothing stands between the bridge and the British. You can hear firing ahead of you now; it is clear that the British have slipped past your position and are near the bridge. Suddenly you spot Spindler and he quickly appraises you of the situation as he understands it. The enemy has broken through to the bridge, but Spindler believes it to be only an initial probing force. He is desperately trying to set up a new defensive line. If you think that the priority is the defensive line you should go to **Decision 229**. If you think it is more important to eliminate the enemy forces before they have had a chance to establish themselves around the bridgehead then go to **Decision 377**.

300

'They're too weak. We need to build up our forces before we can make offensive moves', you tell Spindler. 'Concentrate on the new defence line. I'll do what I can at the bridge.'

Reluctantly you leave the main deployment decisions to Spindler and head for the road bridge. You can see that the forces from the 10th SS are coming, but they are alarmingly weak at the moment. You spot Harder and he tells you that he has already lost his tanks to enemy anti-tank fire. He is carefully watching the enemy, dug in around the bridge ramp, but dare not move forward. If you want to order him to make an attempt to dislodge them then go to **Decision 209**. If you still believe he is too weak to succeed you should go to **Decision 339**.

301

0600 hours 18 September 1944

During the night you hear that the 10th SS has moved towards the ferry crossing at Pannerden. They hope that they will be able to cross here and then approach Nijmegen from the east, as you have ordered. You make the decision to look closely at the defences around Arnhem Bridge and to try to judge the strength of the enemy that has already dug in around those positions.

'Sir, there's armoured movement being reported on the other side of the bridge', Spindler tells you.

Terrible thoughts rush through your mind. It could be the enemy armoured column, but how could they have burst through and overwhelmed Eindhoven and Nijmegen so soon? With great trepidation you raise your binoculars and try to make out the vehicles. You stare for several seconds, trying to figure out what you are watching.

'I think its Graebner', you tell Spindler.

'You're right, he's going to try to rush the bridge!' Spindler replies.

If you want to launch an immediate attack on the northern side of the bridge to support him then go to **Decision 253**. If you prefer to leave the glory to him then go to **Decision 359**.

302

'Where's Division von Tettau?' you wonder. 'What are they doing? They should be pressing the enemy landing zones from the west, get them on the radio', you shout.

With considerable difficulty you make contact with SS Battalion Schultz, tasked with the capture of Renkum to the south of the enemy landing zones. An excited sergeant tells you that they have cleared the town and the terrain to the north of it. Elsewhere it appears that progress is slow, with the hastily-assembled battalions running into considerable opposition. You understand that von Tettau is advancing on an 8km front, with six battalions.

'Get a signal through to the general!' you tell the sergeant. 'We'll give you all possible assistance as soon as we can.'

Now turn to **Decision 255**.

303

1200 hours 18 September 1944

You find Spindler eyeing the defensive ring he has set up around the enemy-held northern ramp and he quickly brings you up to date.

'Von Tettau is launching a series of attacks from the west. We are holding for now. The main effort is to secure the approaches to the northern ramp and launch a series of attacks against the bridgehead. We've established a firm line to the west of Arnhem. At present it is holding despite heavy enemy pressure from the landing zones', he reports.

'Who's making the attacks on the bridgehead?' you ask.

'Knaust and Brinkmann. The enemy hold around eighteen houses.'

If you want to focus on mopping up the bridgehead, go to **Decision 363**. If you want to get a better picture of the situation and head off north-west to check the blocking line then go to **Decision 282**.

304

0900 hours 19 September 1944

You learn that the lead elements of the enemy thrust have crossed a Bailey bridge at Son and just half an hour later they linked up with the Americans at Grave. It is now obvious that the main attack will soon fall on Nijmegen. Decisions have to be made so that you have as complete control of the unfolding events as possible. If you want to contact Model for permission to blow the bridges if they look as if they are about to be captured you should turn to **Decision 388**. If you want to hold firm and hope for the best then go to **Decision 284**.

305

0900 hours 20 September 1944

German counter-attacks are launched all along the corridor. Model has managed to pull together the bulk of the Fifteenth Army. He is feeding the units into the attacks. The situation at Nijmegen is still very dangerous and from your position you can see the enemy preparing for a major attack on the bridges. Still you wait, keeping Model appraised of the situation. At 1300 enemy artillery and tanks begin firing on your positions. They are joined in the attack by rocket-firing Typhoons. They swarm overhead, striking the area and smashing every vehicle or entrenchment they spot. Then you notice small boats on the water. Enemy soldiers are paddling furiously and heading for the northern bank. You stare in horror as they begin to cross, despite their casualties. Then they land. Your forward positions are overwhelmed. Another wave of enemy troops is making for the northern end of the railway bridge. The situation is now desperate.

'General, I urge you to reconsider!' you shout to Model over the radio.

'No! I forbid it!' he tells you.

'But Field Marshal, British tanks are crossing!' you yell.

'Very well, do it', he finally concedes.

Quickly you give the order, but nothing happens. You scream the order again, but there is nothing. The charges must either be defective or the lines to them broken. If you think you should remain here and try and hold them back you should go to **Decision 259**. If you want to retreat you should go to **Decision 345**.

306

1400 hours 19 September 1944

Throughout the night the British paratroopers have been launching attacks all along the blocking line, which have prevented them from breaking through to their fellow airborne troops in the Arnhem Bridge area. So far they have been stopped short of their objectives, but losses are mounting on both sides. Progress by Harmel at the bridge has been slow, but you have taken several prisoners. By 0700 you received news that the enemy armoured column to the south had reached Son and had crossed the river, using a Bailey bridge. Later you learned that all attempts by German forces to stop them pressing forward towards Grave have failed. Little lies between them and Nijmegen. Now turn to **Decision 346**.

307

0730 hours 20 September 1944

Today's reports are very good. The enemy pocket at the bridgehead has been reduced to smouldering ruins. It is estimated that fewer than 300 enemy paratroopers are left. They are short on food and ammunition and must break soon and surrender. The bulk of the enemy forces to the west have been restricted to a series of spoiling attacks along your blocking line. All have been beaten back with heavy casualties. At 1300 you receive alarming news that the enemy is launching a determined attack on Nijmegen. Henke tells you the handful of the 10th SS that have made it to the town are insufficient to hold the enemy off. The signal from Henke is abruptly cut and you pace around your command post, waiting for communication to be re-established with him. Now turn to **Decision 393**.

308

You realise your decision could now mean the difference between success or failure. If the enemy paratroopers are dropping around Arnhem then the whole of your command to the south will be trapped between the enemy armour and the newly landed paratroop reinforcements. It will be another

Falaise Pocket; something you cannot allow to happen. If you want to make the decision to order a retreat over the Arnhem Bridge, go to **Decision 309**. If you think that a single unit sent to investigate will suffice for now you should turn to **Decision 219**.

309

2000 hours 21 September 1944

It now seems clear that the new enemy paratroopers have landed at Driel and are making for the ferry at Heveadorp. You have instructed your units to the south to begin the withdrawal, falling back in stages towards Elst then finally making the last withdrawal over the Arnhem Bridge. This must be achieved by dawn. The morning will bring intense air activity from the enemy and your men will be exposed on the open road. Consulting with Harmel, you decide that many of his support units will head east. They will re-cross the Pannerden Canal and establish a new line. The rest will have to risk the single road towards Arnhem. Meanwhile, you push some of Harzer's more mobile units west to investigate the enemy landings at Driel. Now turn to **Decision 220**.

310

0930 hours 24 September 1944

There has been heavy fighting all around the Oosterbeek bridgehead during the night. At first light the reports begin to come in, suggesting that the enemy has heavily reinforced the bridgehead with at least another brigade of infantry, as well as the Polish paratroopers that landed at Driel. The enemy artillery cover is now virtually complete. Your troops are barely able to move without drawing fire. You curse the missed opportunity. Now you have very few choices, especially as you discover that the enemy has brought up engineers to build a Bailey bridge and is trying to span the Lower Rhine under cover of smoke. At Arnhem the situation is critical, although Model has scraped together some additional reserves. Your ability to hold the bridge is waning, as each salvo of enemy artillery smashes new defensive positions and wrecks all cohesion and order. You know the battle for the Lower Rhine is lost. At 1400 hours this is confirmed when the first elements of the enemy armoured column batter their way across the Arnhem Bridge. Your men continue to desperately resist, but against hopeless odds. Arnhem is lost and with it the door to Germany lays open.

311

1300 hours 23 September 1944

You receive reports that a handful of Polish paratroopers have been slipped across the Rhine during the night. Some supplies have also been sent over, but there is no sign of major activity. With the bulk of the enemy force in the south, still failing to make any headway, you can feel optimistic at the moment. You head back to Doetinchem for a meeting with Field Marshal Model. He demands that you finish off the British airborne troops north of the Rhine within twenty-four hours. He needs the 9th SS to be deployed against the enemy in the south as soon as possible. If you want to go to Oosterbeek and consult with Harzer, go to **Decision 243**. If you want to head to Elst to check the situation on the southern front, go to **Decision 222**.

312

0600 hours 25 September 1944

You hear that some British reinforcements have been ferried across the river during the night. You have also intercepted a partial message from Urquhart, which seems to suggest that they are on the verge of collapse. His communication ended by stating his intention to continue to resist. Now turn to **Decision 291**.

313

The instructions need to be as clear as possible, as they will have to be relayed to the divisions by telephone:

'9SS Pz Div: division is to throw back the enemy, which has already penetrated Arnhem by attacking westwards, and eventually down to the Lower Rhine

10SS Pz Div: division is to attack the enemy forces that have landed by Nijmegen, take possession of the Nijmegen bridges, hold them, and advance to the southern boundary of the town.

It is particularly vital that the Nijmegen enemy forces are prevented from joining those in the north.'

You now begin to work out your coordinating instructions:

'Dividing line between 9SS and 10SS Pz Div is Velp (inclusive to 9SS), the Arnhem road bridge (inclusive to 9SS) and the Lower Rhine towards the west. SS Bn Kraft is already in action directly north of Arnhem towards Oosterbeek within 9SS boundaries, contact is to be established. In exchange for SS Reconnaissance Battalion 9 immediately detached to 10SS, SS Reconnaissance Battalion 10 and one battery of heavy SS Werfer Abteilung 102 (rocket launchers) is to be moved across and taken under command of 9SS. Integrated quick reaction companies under command of 9SS placed under command of Comd Pz Art Regt 9SS Lt-Col Spindler Kampfgruppe. Spindler is to attack along the main east-west thoroughfares through Arnhem towards Oosterbeek. After reaching the western edge of Arnhem he is to form a blocking line between Krafts SS Bn attacking in the north, south to the Lower Rhine. SS Reconnaissance Battalion 10 now referred to as the Kampfgruppe Brinkmann is to attack and destroy the enemy parachute battalion occupying the northern ramp of the Arnhem Bridge. This is in order to quickly establish a resupply route to the 10SS in Nijmegen.'

Model tells you that a scratch unit with the grand name Division von Tettau will be attacking the enemy at Arnhem and Oosterbeek from the west. Kraft's unit is part of this formation, along with a number of other training units and artillerymen being deployed as infantry. Model leaves. Now you need to decide where you will do the most good. You also need to appraise yourself of the situation and the progress of your units. If you want to head for the outskirts of Arnhem then go to **Decision 332**. If you want to make for Arnhem Bridge go to **Decision 245**.

314

You know Henke by sight and spot him barking orders near the main road bridge. You get out of the staff car and he snaps to attention and salutes you.

'Report colonel', you begin.

'Units all alarmed sir, three companies of Ersatz Battalion 6, a company from the Herman Goering training regiment, men from the NCO training school, my regimental staff, some reservists and train guards and police.'

'How many?' you press him.

'750, thereabouts', he replies.

'You need to concentrate on the two bridgeheads Henke', you tell him.

He agrees with you. There are insufficient men here to defend the town.

'Where is the enemy Henke?' you ask.

'Around Zyfflich and Groesbeek, to the south of Nijmegen', he replies.

'Very well', you answer.

If you want to stay here and await your lead elements then go to **Decision 269**. If you want to head back towards Arnhem then turn to **Decision 334**.

315

1700 hours 17 September 1944

'General Kussin is dead!' announces a breathless NCO. 'His aid and driver are killed too.'

'That puts you in command Schliefenbaum', you tell the major.

'Yes sir', he replies, all colour leaving his face. He is clearly petrified.

'Send out vigorous patrols and await reinforcements, they are coming', you promise.

'Yes sir', the major answers.

If you want to head out to find Moeller then go to **Decision 202**. If you want to cross the bridge and make for Nijmegen then go to **Decision 295**.

316

'Get your men forward, Moeller. Engage the enemy', you order.

Moeller salutes and signals for his men to form up. You stand and watch as the scratch battalion moves forward. It has barely advanced 100 metres before it comes under fire. Coming into view is a horde of British paratroopers. You can only be impressed by the flair of the advance and the coordination, as one company detaches itself and makes straight for the railway bridge. Moeller's men are floundering, being cut down and some are running back, hunting for cover. The lead elements of the enemy formation will be there in minutes. If you want to remain and try to stem the tide then go to **Decision 227**. If you would prefer to get out of the area, knowing that the railway bridge is lost, turn to **Decision 354**.

317

There are a series of explosions and then an enormous shock-wave rattles the windows and doors along the street.

'Thank God, the bridge is gone!' you exclaim.

A huge pool of smoke begins to rise beside the river. At least the railway bridge will not fall into enemy hands. Although the bridge is gone, the enemy paratroopers are still moving forward. They seem all the more determined now that only the Arnhem road bridge remains as their objective. Now turn to **Decision 251**.

318

'Graebner, you are to disengage immediately. Do I make myself clear? The Arnhem Bridge is under threat. The 10th cannot cross.'

'Understood. I will disengage as soon as I can', he tells you.

It is all you can ask of him. The worry is that both bridges are in peril at present. Now turn to **Decision 298**.

319

Moeller's men press forward as ordered into withering fire. If anything the enemy is more determined than ever. They know that only the Arnhem road bridge remains. The capture of the bridge will be their salvation; if they fail they will be cut off to the north of the Rhine, and at your mercy. You can see that the enemy is slipping around your flanks. In moments you will either be overwhelmed or surrounded. If you want to order a withdrawal you should turn to **Decision 357**. If you wish to continue to hold them off then go to **Decision 273** .

320

2400 hours 17 September 1944

You drive towards the bridge at Arnhem, acutely aware of the dangerous situation. You have the 9th SS building up and making for Arnhem, but your plan to slip the 10th SS across the road bridge seems to have faded at present. Without reserves it looks as if you will have to rely on Henke alone to defend Nijmegen. You can see the situation for yourself; Harder's men are struggling to form a line near the bridge. Even now there are rumours that the British are massing and intend to overwhelm the new defensive perimeter around the northern approach. Now turn to **Decision 301**.

321

'Focus on holding the line. Keep pressing around the bridge if possible. If the enemy establishes in Arnhem in any force then we're finished', you tell Spindler.

'I fear they are already here in force, sir. The pressure to the west from the landing zones has dissipated. I suspect the bulk of his men are already in position', Spindler replies.

'No doubt he will attempt to land reinforcements today', you reason.

'Then the landing zones are still the key', Spindler suggests.

If you think this is the case then go to **Decision 302**. If you think Spindler is wrong you should turn to **Decision 340**.

322

'Push forward and link up with Graebner. Give him all your support', you order.

You are in a dangerous situation. Any minute now the enemy could easily overwhelm your positions and take the bridge. Options are diminishing. If you want to continue to resist as best you can, go to **Decision 383**. If you want to order the Arnhem Bridge to be blown, go to **Decision 213**.

323

'Fall back Spindler, north, otherwise we'll be trapped', you order.

Spindler immediately signals the withdrawal. It is a costly one; only handfuls of men manage to get themselves out of the trap. It takes several hours for the situation to become clearer. The bulk of the 10th SS has headed for Pannerden, leaving you with scratch units in the north of Arnhem. With the decrease in pressure on your side of the landing areas von Tettau has made virtually no progress in the west. Above all, the Arnhem bridges are now in the hands of the enemy. Now turn to **Decision 362**.

324

As you signal for your staff car you can already predict that the attack will end in failure. There has to be another option. The 9th SS has to press the northern ramp, but why the lack of progress? The 10th need to make a determined effort to get to Nijmegen, otherwise that too will be lost. If you want to make for Nijmegen, go to **Decision 343**. If you want to try to get to Arnhem by the east you should turn to **Decision 303**.

325

'Bittrich you are relieved of command. I will take control of the situation myself. Put Henke on the line and, as for you, you are to report to Berlin. We will deal with your cowardice and insubordination at a court martial', Model orders you.

Your command of the corps and your military career is over.

326

'Attack the new landings, throw everything you have at them', you order your officers.

You know that coordinating the attacks and getting the men into position will take time, but time is something that you do not have. Suddenly a staff car pulls up beside your command post and Field Marshal Model steps out. You quickly explain the situation and tell him how dangerous this new development has become.

'Call off the assault', he tells you. 'Besides, I am sure you are going to demand the blowing of the Nijmegen bridges too.'

If you do indeed want to argue with his orders, go to **Decision 238**. If you broadly agree with him you should turn to **Decision 239**.

327

0730 hours 20 September 1944

Harmel tells you that there is little to report. He has arranged for what remains of Graebner's unit to keep an eye on the southern bank of the river. He has identified two possibilities; either a landing near Elden or perhaps at Driel. The enemy pocket at the bridgehead has been reduced to smouldering ruins. It is estimated that fewer than 300 enemy paratroopers are left. They are short on food and ammunition and must break soon and surrender. The bulk of the enemy forces to the west have been restricted to a series of spoiling attacks along your blocking line. All have been beaten back with heavy casualties. At 1300 you receive alarming news that the enemy is launching a determined attack on Nijmegen. Henke tells you the handful of the 10th SS that have made it to the town are insufficient to hold the enemy off. The signal from Henke is abruptly cut and you pace around your command post, waiting for communication to be re-established with him. Now turn to **Decision 393**.

328

Trapped in a pocket of your own making, you eagerly await news and reinforcement. Reports from the south are depressing; Nijmegen has fallen, the 10th SS is scattered, and what remains of the 9th SS is too feeble to assist you. The enemy paratroopers have continued to harass you and surround the bridgehead.

You receive a handful of reinforcements; partial scratch units that have fled from the south. They are poorly equipped, exhausted and of little use and are just more mouths to feed. Towards 2000 hours you hear the rumble of vehicles approaching the bridge from the south. More in hope than anything else, you dream that it is reinforcements and you can break out of the pocket. Your hopes are dashed as you see the first vehicle emerge from the gathering darkness; it is a Sherman tank. Behind it is an endless column of vehicles. There is little point in trying to resist. You wrap your handkerchief around your swagger stick and gingerly walk forward to offer your surrender.

329

0600 hours 22 September 1944

You are already checking the defence lines and observing enemy movement over the river when a signal from Field Marshal Model gets through to you: 'Bittrich, I understand you have surrendered the ground between Nijmegen and Arnhem. Is that correct?'

'Yes Field Marshal I …'

'Cowardice Bittrich, of the worst kind! You have surrendered precious land without cause and imperilled Germany. You have not even managed to eliminate the British on the north of the Rhine have you?'

'No, Field Marshal, but ….'

'But nothing! You are relieved of command. Put Harzer on the line. He has the steel nerve that we need. As for you, report immediately to Berlin and expect to have answers to some very searching questions!'

Your command of the corps is over and your military career is in tatters.

330

1400 hours 22 September 1944

You drive as close to Driel as you dare. From your vantage point you can see a small British armoured force racing for the river. There are tanks and trucks and a handful of amphibious vehicles. The force is insufficient to make any great difference to the situation on the northern side of the river. You can only assume that the column aims to either resupply the British paratroopers or to try to evacuate the wounded. The amphibious craft could be used to ferry reinforcements across, but nowhere near enough to tip the balance. If you want to return to Arnhem then go to **Decision 221**. If you want to drive on to Elst then go to **Decision 265**.

331

2100 hours 25 September 1944

Your units report that the enemy artillery is pounding their positions. There are also enemy units further west firing over the Rhine. You fear it might be another attempt to force the river. Quickly you make for Oosterbeek to check the situation. Now turn to **Decision 400**.

332

As you run for your staff car you see your motorcycle escort readying themselves to move off to protect you. You wonder how much use they will be should you come under enemy air attack. The enemy's air superiority is undoubted and your men suffered greatly from it in France and throughout the retreat through Belgium and into Holland. You drive up the road from Doetinchen to Dieren, watching the gun flashes and more parachute drops way-off to the south-west, around Nijmegen. Your route will take you along the banks of the Lower Rhine, through Rhedn and Velp, approaching Arnhem from the west, south of the bridge. During the journey you pass scattered units of your command, the 9th SS heading towards Arnhem and the 10th towards Nijmegen. Once you get to Arnhem you will have a choice. You can either head north over the bridge and go to **Decision 351**, or you can swing south towards Nijmegen and go to **Decision 372**.

333

'We've little time', you tell Schliefenbaum, 'I've ordered a reconnaissance unit to pass through here. The 9th SS is *en route*. Meanwhile we'll have to make the best of it. Where is Moeller's battalion?'

Moeller commands upwards of eighty engineers and is part of the 9th SS. He would have been one of the first to get to Arnhem.

'Around the Elizabeth Hospital area, on the Utrechtseweg towards Oosterbeek. I believe they are engaged with the enemy', the major replies.

If you want to remain at the bridge and see what can be done to repair the defences then go to **Decision 315**. If you would prefer to find Moeller then go to **Decision 202**.

334

You get back in your staff car, confident at the moment that the enemy is not seriously threatening Nijmegen. The return journey is uneventful, but it worries you that there is still no sign of any of your units ordered to make for Nijmegen. You can only hope that the situation at the Arnhem Bridge is better. Suddenly an aircraft appears overhead, and clearly it is an enemy fighter. Your driver swerves off the road and hugs the tree line, in the hope that you will not be spotted. The driver stops momentarily, waiting for the aircraft to disappear. Now turn to **Decision 352**.

335

You hope that the Nijmegen situation is stable for the time being. Soon the 10th will be here, but you worry why it is taking them so long. If you can prevent the enemy in Arnhem from linking up with those around Nijmegen then they can be picked off at your leisure. You begin your drive back towards Arnhem, noting with satisfaction that Graebner has had the sense to leave some half-tracks and anti-tank guns near Elst. This will ensure that he remains in radio contact with the 9th SS in Arnhem. As you approach the Arnhem Bridge you can see that one of Graebner's half-track reconnaissance groups is in action at the southern end of the bridge. They are exchanging fire with the enemy in some houses along the northern bank. A real crisis is looming here; perhaps the enemy is about to overwhelm the bridge at Arnhem. If you want to get a closer look then go to **Decision 336**. If you want to order Graebner to get back to Arnhem immediately and force the bridge then go to **Decision 205**.

336

You order the driver to proceed towards the southern ramp. The firing is scattered and not intense, but it is clear that the enemy is gathering in strength on the opposite bank.

'We're in contact with Kampfgruppe Reinhold', an SS captain tells you.

'Yes, and?' you reply.

'His lead elements are pinned down to the north of the bridge. The bulk of the rest of the division is making for the crossing at Pannerden.'

'That's the ferry isn't it?' you ask.

'Yes sir, but it is going to take time for them to get there and to get across.'

If you want to order the reconnaissance group to try and get across the bridge then go to **Decision 355**. If you want to make for Pannerden and check the ferry crossing you should turn to **Decision 228**.

337

1830 hours 17 September 1944

The bridge is lost and Moeller's men have been overwhelmed. As you approach the Arnhem road bridge the situation looks bleak.

'Where are the 10th SS?' you wonder.

In answer to your question you begin seeing small units of German troopers. It must be Spindler, but you cannot help wondering if he is too late. Spindler's core of his Kampfgruppe is two depleted companies of his own armoured artillery regiment. They have no heavy weapons and there are just 120 of them. As you proceed you see Spindler himself. His main task was to help establish a blocking line and he appears to have been scraping up scattered units.

'Report Lieutenant Colonel', you demand.

'The enemy is everywhere, sir. They've taken some houses near the north ramp of the bridge, as far as we can tell. We are gathering up all the fighting groups that we can and trying to set up a defensive line to keep the main enemy force at bay.'

If you want to focus on the blocking line then go to **Decision 229**. If you think it more important to cut off the enemy at the bridge then you should go to **Decision 377**.

338

2400 hours 17 September 1944

By the close of the day the news is more promising. Harder has succeeded in forming a new blocking line in the western suburbs of Arnhem. He can now deny access to the bridge, which is some 800m from his main positions. Despite this, the British 1 Parachute Brigade is still trying to punch its way through.

'You are the main point of defence Spindler', you tell him. 'Is there any word about Allworden?'

'None, sir. I fear the enemy may have overwhelmed him', he replies.

Now turn to **Decision 252**.

339

'We simply do not have enough men', you tell Harder. 'Tell your men to stand down and to return to their defensive positions. I think we're better off waiting. You must make sure that you deny the enemy the chance to reinforce his bridge area. This is all we can hope for at the moment.'

Harder looks relieved and agrees with you. Even as you turn away you wonder if you have not missed an opportunity here. Your other key concern is that the enemy can also slip men across the river and, perhaps, threaten the southern end of the bridge. At the moment there is nothing that you can do about it. Now turn to **Decision 301**.

340

'That's von Tettau's concern', you tell Spindler. 'We've got more important things to deal with. I'm heading for the bridge. Brinkmann's kampfgruppe has been tasked to storm the bridge.'

By the time you get there you can see Brinkmann has already committed his men. They are engaged in vicious close-quarter fighting with the enemy. You watch as Brinkmann's reconnaissance battalion tries an armoured rush. A column of light tanks, armoured cars and half-tracks clatter under the bridge ramp and burst into Markt-Straad. They are met with withering fire, a pair of British 6pdrs that are bringing the lead tank to a blazing halt. The German half-tracks try to get around but they are knocked out one by one. The troopers baling out are cut down. The whole thing is uncoordinated. You know it is a failure. This attempt has clearly ended in disaster. Now you hear armoured movement on the other side of the bridge. Spindler has rejoined you.

'I think it's Graebner', he tells you.

'He's going to try and rush the bridge', you reply.

If you want to launch an immediate attack to support Graebner then go to **Decision 253**. If you think he can achieve it alone you should turn to **Decision 359**.

341

0600 hours 18 September 1944

At dawn Brinkmann attempted to rush the northern ramp of the Arnhem Bridge, following a barrage of artillery and mortar fire. Unfortunately it was an uncoordinated attack and although the fighting is continuing it appears to have ended in failure.

'It is imperative that we take the bridge back. They only hold the northern ramp don't they?' you ask.

'The bridge, yes, Graebner is planning to attack from the south as soon as he can', Spindler tells you.

There have to be other options to get the 10th SS to Nijmegen. It seems like someone has already been looking into this and you receive a signal that engineers have been sent to Pannerden to try and sort out the ferry. You decide to make for the ferry crossing to check the situation and see what options are available. As you reach there you see lead elements of the 10th SS Engineer Battalion. They signal you from the other side of the canal. You can already see that progress is going to be slow and it will be very difficult to get vehicles across the ferry. Now turn to **Decision 254**.

342

It is a catastrophic failure. Spindler's men are being overwhelmed. Sporadic attempts to counter-attack are beaten back with huge losses. The enemy is adding artillery fire and mortar rounds to the confusion and carnage. Surviving SS troopers are beginning to flee and the new danger is that you will be captured. If you want to order a retreat to the north, go to **Decision 323**. If you want to remain and try to salvage the situation you should go to **Decision 384**.

343

1200 hours 18 September 1944

'Where's the enemy now?' you demand, as you walk up to Henke.

'Reports suggest he is in strength around Groesbeek, to the south-east of Nijmegen. He is probing towards the town', Henke tells you.

'And the enemy main thrust from the south?' you ask.

'Eindhoven', he replies.

'So there's still time', you figure. 'It will still take time for the 10th to get here.'

'A company of engineers is already here from the division', Henke tells you.

'Good. The corps directive is for them to prepare both bridges for demolition. However, we need the express authority of the field marshal to fire the charges', you reply.

An SS captain strides up to you.

'Euling, sir, reporting with a hundred men. I'm with Kampfgruppe Reinhold', he reports.

He explains that he crossed the Lower Rhine at Huissen and made his way here via Elst. If you want to order him to establish a bridgehead to the south of the Waal then go to **Decision 257**. If you think he is better served as a reserve for now you should turn to **Decision 235**.

344

1800 hours 18 September 1944

It takes you some time to get to Arnhem, but as you approach from the east you make sure you do not stray too close to the northern approach to the bridge. The situation at the bridge appears stable for now. Spindler has set up a blocking line to prevent the enemy at the ramp from being reinforced. Meanwhile, Division von Tettau in the west has been launching attacks on the enemy landing zones. If you want to check the situation around the landing zones then go to **Decision 282**. If you want to focus on the bridge you should go to **Decision 363**.

345

You continually stop and observe as you fall back along the road running beside the railway line. You can see British tanks nosing towards Lent. Incredibly, they seem to stop.

'Why aren't they pushing on to Elst?' you wonder.

You might still be able to salvage some kind of victory here, from the shambles of Nijmegen. Now turn to **Decision 389**.

346

1530 hours 19 September 1944

Harzer has gathered his tanks and artillery to pound every building around the Arnhem bridgehead, still being held by the enemy. Tiger tanks prowl the streets of Arnhem, searching for scattered groups of enemy paratroopers. You hear alarming news that fresh British paratroopers landed yesterday to the north-west of Arnhem. Intelligence suggests that three fresh battalions of the enemy are now pressing east and threatening the blocking line. There must be more enemy reinforcements on the way, as undoubtedly they believe that the pendulum has swung in their direction. It seems to you that the next logical step for the enemy would be to try to land paratroopers on the south of the river and to take the bridge. If you could order a blocking force to get there first then this would prevent that. If you wish to do this you should turn to **Decision 218**. If you think it unlikely then go to **Decision 307**.

347

'Harmel, pull out. Head north if you can', you tell him.

'Sir, we are under heavy artillery fire and the enemy is advancing under cover of their barrage', he shouts back over the radio.

'Get out before you are destroyed!' you beg him.

Several minutes pass but Harmel contacts you again and is able to report that he has managed to extricate his command. Harzer's battered 9th SS is crossing the Arnhem Bridge and establishing a defensive ring around the southern approach to the bridge. News from Arnhem and Oosterbeek is very promising. The bulk of the enemy force still active to the north of the river has been boxed into a position around Oosterbeek. The line protecting Arnhem has held out and von Tettau is pressing hard from the west. Nonetheless you need to consider what to do with Harmel. The options are limited. He can either remain in position off to the east as a threat to the enemy if they try and force their way towards Elst and Arnhem, in which case you should turn to **Decision 367**. Alternatively you could order them to manoeuvre through Bemmel and Ressen and make for the road leading to Arnhem via Elst, in which case you should go to **Decision 240**.

348

It is a terrible slaughter, reminiscent of the worst defeats in France. The whole area is littered with burning vehicles as Harmel's troops are mercilessly pounded by artillery and harried by enemy fighter-bombers. Belatedly you push Kampfgruppe Knaust over the bridge to race to Elst to cover the retreat that has turned into a rout. Harmel is missing in action. He could be dead or captured but no one seems to know. Precious few of his men make it back to the bridge and the comparative safety of Arnhem. Scattered units still appear throughout the night and the enemy has surged forward to claim the abandoned ground. Now turn to **Decision 329**.

349

1200 hours 23 September 1944

Confused reports are coming in. It is clear that the enemy has now reached Elden and is laying fire down on your positions around the Arnhem Bridge. The intensity of the fire is increasing hour by hour. At Oosterbeek the opinions from your commanders on the ground seem to suggest that the enemy is either trying to reinforce the British airborne troops north of the river in force, or they are mounting an evacuation. The 9th SS is still pressing from the east and von Tettau from the west. Progress reports indicate that your men are slowly gaining ground, but coming under increased artillery fire from the enemy on the southern bank of the river. You know you cannot afford to allow the enemy to reinforce north of the river. It will pin down the bulk of your available forces and it will compromise your ability to defend the Arnhem Bridge. If you want to throw everything you have at the Oosterbeek bridgehead now, go to **Decision 290**. If you think a gradual pressing action is all that is necessary, go to **Decision 310**.

350

1600 hours 24 September 1944

You receive news just before 1600 that elements of the 9th SS have established contact with lead units of von Tettau's forces in the west; effectively the pocket is now sealed. The junction was made near the gasworks by the river itself. Despite all enemy attempts to stop you, the British paratroopers are now surrounded and cut off from the river. If you want to order the pocket to be reduced, which might take time, go to **Decision 244**. If you wish to call on the enemy to surrender, go to **Decision 396**.

351

1600 hours 17 September 1944

The outskirts of Arnhem are attractive. There are neat houses and gardens, cobbled roadways, tarmac drives and bicycle tracks. As you see the bridge it is readily apparent that it is thinly held. You stop at the northern ramp.

'Where's Major General Kussin?" you demand. Kussin is responsible for the defence of the road bridge.

'He is out briefing and advising other units sir', answers Kussin's chief-of-staff, Major Schliefenbaum.

'You are responsible that we hold Arnhem until the major general reappears', you reply.

The major nods, but guarding the bridge are just two dozen elderly men and teenagers, manning a light flak battery around the bridge. There are very few other soldiers here. Understandably you are alarmed. If you wish to stay here and organise a proper defence of the bridge then go to **Decision 333**. If you want to drive on and find your own lead units in Arnhem then go to **Decision 202**.

352

Several minutes pass and there is no sign of the enemy aircraft. You can continue on your way, making for the Arnhem Bridge. When you arrive you see little sign of preparation; only a handful of elderly men and teenagers are manning a flak unit near the bridge. A few more security men are standing beside a bunker. You get out of the car and a major walks over and salutes you.

'Schliefenbaum, major general Kussin's chief of staff', he introduces himself.

'Where's Kussin?' you ask.

'He's out advising units in Arnhem sir'.

You nod. Things are not exactly as you expected. There are no signs of your lead units from 9th SS. If you want to remain here and help to organise the defence then go to **Decision 333**. If you want to go into Arnhem and find your lead units then go to **Decision 202**.

353

The lance corporal is shocked to see you. He snaps to attention and introduces himself as Buttler.

'We've been in a running fight with British paratroopers. My men are infantry and artillery from the 10th SS, sir. We were cut off from the rest of the division in the retreat from France. We were having a quick lunch when the airborne landings began at Oosterbeek.'

'Who are the enemy?' you demand.

British 2nd Parachute Battalion. We held them up for a while at the Oosterbeek–Laag railway station, but there were too many of them', he tells you.

'How far behind you?' you ask.

'Minutes, sir, perhaps less.'

If you want to coordinate the defences here then go to **Decision 296**. If you want to personally supervise the destruction of the bridge then go to **Decision 248**.

354

'Just hold them Moeller as long as you can, buy us some time,' you tell him as you get into your staff car.

'You can rely on us', he tells you.

Frankly you doubt he will be able to hold on for much longer. You take one last look at the onrushing enemy paratroopers and then tap the driver on the shoulder.

'Arnhem Bridge', you order.

Now turn to **Decision 337**.

355

'Lieutenant, get your men ready. I want to make a dash across the bridge, clear it and link up with the 10th SS', you order him.

The lieutenant salutes and begins assembling his small force. They are under continuous fire now, with the occasional mortar round landing near the southern ramp of the bridge. At least there is only one bridge to worry about at Arnhem. But its solitary existence makes it all the more important. It takes a few minutes for the men to mount up in the four half-tracks. They are now ready for action. If you want to join them in the attack go to **Decision 250**. If you want to watch the attack from the south bank you should go to **Decision 356**.

356

The half-tracks start up and rumble onto the southern ramp. As they drive up the bridge towards the centre all seems well. But then they pass out of sight, as they cross over the middle of the bridge to begin their descent towards the northern ramp. All of a sudden there is a single explosion nearby and then it is joined by intense machine-gun fire. Mortar shells plop around the bridge area then you see smoke and flames reaching into the skies. The cacophony of sound reaches a crescendo and then there is silence. Now turn to **Decision 211**.

357

'Save your men, Moeller', you order, clambering into a staff car. 'Fall back. At least the railway bridge is useless to them.'

'We need support now and besides we'll lose contact with the anti-aircraft unit nearest the river and Kraft's men to the north', says Moeller.

'I know that', you tell him.

If you want the order to stand then go to **Decision 378**. If you want to order the whole line back, go to **Decision 275**.

358

2400 hours 17 September 1944

You can only hope that the situation at the bridge is better. It becomes increasingly clear that the enemy has slipped past Moeller by way of the riverbank. They have established themselves in Arnhem, near the northern ramp. You spot Spindler talking to some other officers. He looks worried but is obviously working tirelessly to organise his men.

'We've established a broad front', he begins, spreading out a map on the table of a requisitioned Dutch house. 'Kraft is on the Ede-Arnhem Road, Gropp is at the railway cutting, then Moeller. My own companies are covering the gap now on the Lower Rhine. We're feeding units in as they arrive.'

'What about the bridge?' you demand

'SS Kampfgruppe Harder is holding the perimeter around the bridge area. Communication is difficult. Despatch riders are being picked off by enemy snipers. We are having to use armoured vehicles in order to make sure that messages get through.'

'You've done very well Spindler, but the bridge area has to be cleared', you tell him.

'Yes. Fighting has died down for now. We can expect renewed attempts to break through from the enemy in the morning.'

Now turn to **Decision 341**.

359

You stare in fascination as Graebner's reconnaissance force rumbles forward. He has a mix of armoured cars, half-tracks and lorries, the latter covered in sandbags to provide his men with some protection. Graebner's lead elements reach the centre point of the bridge before you hear any firing. You know how painfully exposed they are and that they can only come on virtually one after the next. Suddenly Graebner's force opens fire. The lead Pumas fire into the buildings around the northern ramp; for a moment it looks as if they are going to make it. Then the British open fire with PIATs, mortars and Bren guns; resistance is fierce from the enemy paratroopers. You see one Puma after another burst into flames. Still the firing goes on. Next in line for the punishing treatment are the half-tracks. The enemy throws in grenades to the open fighting-compartments and shoots PIAT rounds. Black smoke boils up as blazing fuel engulfs the crews of the half-tracks. Graebner's attack begins to disintegrate. The SS troopers desperately seek refuge amongst the slaughter. Now turn to **Decision 379**.

360

A series of mortar rounds straddle the bridge. One of the half-tracks is hit squarely in the open compartment. The men inside disappear in smoke and flames. Another series of explosions lands close to your half-track, bursting the tyres. The driver struggles to keep control of the vehicle, but loses the battle and it hits one of the support girders. The jarring impact stuns you and you can feel blood trickling down your face. You pass out, mercifully not witnessing the PIAT round that hits the half-track and reduces it to a blazing inferno.

361

The lead elements of the 10th SS Engineer Battalion have arrived at the ferry crossing. They signal to you that work is already under way. Immediately you can see that the progress is going to be slow. It will be incredibly difficult to get the vehicles across. You can only hope that Graebner's attack is a success and that the Arnhem Bridge can be used instead. Now turn to **Decision 254**.

362

0600 hours 18 September 1944

With the 9th SS in tatters and the 10th out to the south–east your options are very limited. Radio contact with von Tettau is sporadic and you cannot raise Henke at Nijmegen. The worry is that the enemy will now try to land reinforcements on the uncontested landing zones. This will tip the balance permanently in the favour of the allies to an irretrievable degree. You fear that the battle is already lost. With reluctance you contact Field Marshal Model and explain the situation to him. He is furious and blames you for the loss of the bridges:

'You are relieved of your command, Bittrich. I will personally take control of the situation. Report to Berlin immediately. There will be a court martial. Your command of the Corps is over.'

363

Harmel has arrived from Berlin. You quickly update him. He will take his 10th SS south to secure Nijmegen. Harzer will deal with the British here in Arnhem.

'How am I to get my units to Nijmegen?' he asks.

You explain that ferrying operations have already begun. He also wonders why the bridges at Nijmegen have not yet been destroyed. You shrug and explain to him that the Field Marshal wants to retain them for counterattacks. You can see from the expression on his face that he knows there are no available units to launch any counterattacks. All you can do is to agree with him. There is little left. Now turn to **Decision 365**.

364

You decide to throw all of Reinhold's kampfgruppe across the river. But even now you can see enemy tanks moving up towards the bridge. There is a desperate battle by the riverside, as both sides feed in men and machines. You immediately realise that your error in holding back for so long means there are simply too many of the enemy. You dare not blow the bridges, as only Model can order their destruction. All you can hope is that sufficient forces remain to take them back. The depleted and dispirited elements of your command are crushed against the bridgehead. You know the bridges are lost. You can now only focus on Arnhem and hope to retrieve the situation. You pull back towards Elst and receive a radio signal direct from Model:

'You are relieved of your command Bittrich. I will personally take control of the situation. Report to Berlin immediately. You will be court martialled. Your command of the corps is over.'

365

1400 hours 18 September 1944

You receive an alert that fresh landings have been made by the enemy to the north-west of Arnhem, at Ginkel Heath. The reports suggest that it is at least a brigade-strength landing and some three full battalions of British paratroopers have arrived. Dutch SS in the area have fled and have been scattered. Von Tettau is still attempting to advance in the west and you learn, to your relief, that Harmel is still holding at present. An hour-or-so later, Model visits your command post. Again you ask about the destruction of the Nijmegen bridges.

'The answer is no if you mean to destroy them', he tells you. 'Student's First Parachute Army will hold the enemy back at Nijmegen. Even now the Fifteenth Army is mustering to make attacks along the enemy airborne corridor. You have 24 hours to retake the bridge at Arnhem. What is holding you back?'

If you want to argue with Model then go to **Decision 238**. If you want to obey orders then go to **Decision 306**.

366

0600 hours 21 September 1944

This decision means that Harmel's 10th SS is too far south and east to be of much use to you. Harzer's battered 9th SS is crossing the Arnhem Bridge and establishing a defensive ring around the southern approach to the bridge. News from Arnhem and Oosterbeek is very promising. The bulk of the enemy force still active to the north of the river has been boxed into a position around Oosterbeek. The line protecting Arnhem has held out and von Tettau is pressing hard from the west. Nonetheless you need to consider what to do with Harmel. The options are limited. He can remain in position off to the east as a threat to the enemy if they try and force their way towards Elst and Arnhem, in which case you should turn to **Decision 367**. Alternatively you could order them to manoeuvre through Bemmel and Ressen and make for the road leading to Arnhem via Elst, in which case you should go to **Decision 240**.

367

1100 hours 21 September 1944

You receive reports that the enemy armoured column has begun its drive on Arnhem. Buzzing overhead of the lead elements of the column are dozens of Typhoon fighter-bombers. At Oosterbeek, although the enemy is surrounded, they are now in range of the armoured column's artillery support. You begin receiving reports that your units pressing the British 1st Airborne are taking heavy casualties from the bombardments. By 1700 hours there is even more disquieting news; in fact you can see it for yourself. Literally dozens of enemy Spitfires have appeared overhead. They seem to be concentrating on your positions to the west of the southern approach to the Arnhem Bridge. There are reports of mass attacks by fighters on a number of positions. The reason for the interest in this area becomes alarmingly obvious; the sky is filling with enemy bombers and transport aircraft. Your anti-aircraft units engage them as they come into range. Suddenly you see parachutes in the sky, hundreds of them.

'Driel! They're dropping on Driel! They mean to outflank us!' you hear over the radio.

If you think this is the case and want to retreat over the Arnhem Bridge you should go to **Decision 368**. If you think this is nonsense, go to **Decision 241**.

368

You order the retreat across the Arnhem Bridge, back the way your men came, having lost so many men and so much blood. But you see no other option. You try and remain in radio contact with Harmel. He is now even further south-east and out of the battle. You tell him to attack the enemy armoured columns if they try to exploit the clear ground between Nijmegen and the Arnhem Bridge.

'I doubt whether we can deploy in time', he tells you.

He is right, and besides that being on the western side of the Pannerden Canal could potentially mean that he will be trapped if the enemy resumes the advance.

'Pull back across the canal. Destroy the ferry and hold a new line to the east of the canal', you order him.

You re-establish your defences to the north of the Arnhem Bridge, but then reports begin to come in. It is apparent that the enemy paratroopers are not threatening the bridge at all. They have landed at Driel and are more intent on capturing the ferry at Heveadorp. Your retreat has created a vacuum that the enemy armoured column in the south is happy to fill. Already they have reached Elst and are probing north-west to link up with the newly arrived paratroopers at Driel. It is a disaster. By morning the enemy will have secured all the ground south of the Lower Rhine. Now turn to **Decision 329**.

369

0830 hours 23 September 1944

There is little in the way of new developments. An attempt by enemy paratroopers on the south of the river to cross to the north has failed. The bulk of supplies being flown in by the enemy to the north of the Rhine have fallen into your hands. Everyone has English cigarettes and American chocolate. One more push against the enemy on the northern bank should finish them off.

Field Marshal Model arrives at your command post: 'I want a quick finish. I need your men for the counter-offensive south. You have 24 hours to finish them off. Time is of the essence Bittrich', he tells you.

You understand what he is saying to you, but the enemy has moved up to Elst and your positions are under continuous artillery fire. You dare not ask about the demolition of the bridge. Simply, the British need to be destroyed here on the northern bank of the river. No sooner has Model left than you hear of developments near Driel. The situation is confused. If you wish to investigate then go to **Decision 264**. If you are content to let the local commanders handle the situation and keep you informed, go to **Decision 349**.

370

2400 hours 22 September 1944

After issuing a stream of orders, confused reports arrive. It is clear that the enemy has now reached Elden and have opened fire on your positions around the Arnhem Bridge. At Oosterbeek the opinions from your commanders on the ground seem to suggest that the enemy is either trying to reinforce the British airborne troops north of the river in force, or they are mounting an evacuation. The 9th SS is still pressing from the east and von Tettau from the west. Progress reports indicate that your men are slowly gaining ground, but coming under increased artillery fire from the enemy on the southern bank of the river. You know you cannot afford to allow the enemy to reinforce north of the river: it will pin down the bulk of your available forces and it will compromise your ability to defend the Arnhem Bridge. If you want to throw everything you have at the Oosterbeek bridgehead now, go to **Decision 290**. If you think a gradual pressing action is all that is necessary, go to **Decision 310**.

371

1900 hours 24 September 1944

With some difficulty you get a message through to Urquhart, requesting his surrender. The reply is prompt and terse. He declines without question. It is clear that this is either bravado from a beaten enemy, or that indeed the enemy intends to reinforce. Perhaps he is just playing for time? Now turn to **Decision 397**.

372

1600 hours 17 September 1944

You approach the outskirts of Arnhem, the Pannerden Canal is to your left, heading for the River Waal. The roads are clear of German traffic. There is little sign of the battle except for the occasional flash of gunfire to the south beyond Nijmegen. You can only hope that Nijmegen Bridge is being held by Colonel Henke, who is commander of the Nijmegen Defence Force. You know he has only some small units of paratroopers, trainees and reservists. You skirt Elst at the railway crossing and continue south, re-crossing the railway just outside of Nijmegen. Now turn to **Decision 314**.

373

'Where's the demolition party?' you ask Moeller.

'On the south side of the river, an NCO and ten men billeted in some houses near the bridge', he replies.

'Tell them to blow the bridge, Moeller', you order him.

You can hear firing from the direction of Oosterbeek. There must be small units of German soldiers ahead. Suddenly you see three lorries heading along the road close to the river, making for Oosterbeek. In horror you watch as khaki clad soldiers surround the vehicles. There is more firing; this time along the northern railway embankment. A handful of German stragglers emerge, all dressed in camouflage smocks. A war-worn SS lance corporal leads them. Now turn to **Decision 353**.

374

A 10th SS man, Lance Corporal Buttler, lopes into view at the head of a handful of SS men in camouflage smocks. He salutes and begins to report: 'Hundreds of British paratroopers just behind us.'

'What are you doing here lance corporal, why aren't you with your division?' you demand.

'Cut off, sir, during the retreat from France. We were making our way to division when the landings started', he explains.

'Where are the enemy exactly?' you question him.

'Heading this way, sir, they mean to capture the bridges, I am sure of it', he tells you.

'Clearly', you reply.

Perhaps you should order the bridge to be blown? If you think so go to **Decision 248**. If you think this is an unnecessary panic then go to **Decision 271**.

375

'Graebner I want you to get back here as soon as possible, turn around', you tell him over the radio.

'It's difficult. We are already engaged', he tells you.

Perhaps it is too late to change your plans. You think through the options but there is little else that you can do, except to order Graebner back and risk allowing the Americans the initiative at Nijmegen. Now turn to **Decision 205**.

376

2400 hours 17 September 1944

There has to be other options to get the 10th SS to Nijmegen. It seems like someone has already been looking into this and you receive a signal that engineers have been sent to Pannerden to try and sort out the ferry. You decide to make for the ferry crossing to check the situation and see what options are available. As you reach there you see lead elements of the 10th SS Engineer Battalion. They signal you from the other side of the canal. You can already see that progress is going to be slow and it will be very difficult to get vehicles across the ferry. Now turn to **Decision 254**.

377

'Who's closer to the bridge Spindler?' you ask.

'Harder, sir', he replies.

'What's his strength?'

'He's only got three scratch companies and three Panthers, if they are still operational', Spindler answers.

If you want to send Harder's command towards the bridge then go to **Decision 338**. If you think they are too weak to make any difference you should go to **Decision 300**.

378

'Just fall back, Moeller, before it is too late', you tell him.

It is a dangerous choice but you cannot let Moeller's men be cut down in what is obviously a lost cause. He begins ordering what remains of his command to fall back, section by section. The whole area seems alive with the enemy. You hope that elements of either the 9th or the 10th have begun to deploy behind you. If they have failed to do so then there will be a certainty that the enemy will capture the road bridge at Arnhem. If you want to remain and help Moeller to organise the withdrawal then go to **Decision 273**. If you would rather make for the bridge then go to **Decision 358**.

379

SS troopers leap over the balustrades of the bridge and into the Lower Rhine, rather than face the withering fire. Slowly the firing dies down, only to start up again from an unexpected quarter. Bursting into view from the river bank is a large, determined group of enemy paratroopers. They catch Spindler's unprepared units and begin overwhelming them. The situation is incredibly dangerous. If you want to launch a counter-attack you should turn to **Decision 279**. If you want to order an immediate withdrawal then go to **Decision 323**.

380

0900 hours 18 September 1944

Graebner is a flamboyant character, and is much loved by his men. He is an impressive soldier; everything a commander of a reconnaissance unit needs to be – brave and resourceful. Supporting the 277th Infantry Division in Normandy, he led a series of counter-attacks against British breakthroughs at Noyers Bocage in July 1944. At dawn on 15 July he overran an allied penetration and averted a crisis. This had won him the Ritterkreuz, or Knight's Cross.

'Surprise and shock Graebner, that's what we have', you tell him.

He agrees. He has twenty-two armoured vehicles at his disposal. There is a mix of armoured cars and half-tracks and some of them have 75mm guns. The rest of the command is made up of trucks, with heavy sandbags for protection. This is the highest concentration of armoured vehicles in the 9th SS. The engines are revving and the whole column is partially shrouded in exhaust fumes. They begin forming up into an attack column. There is a rush of some 700m up the ramp then another 200m across the span and then down, into Arnhem. The armoured cars will lead. If you want to go ahead and be part of this attack, go to **Decision 234**. If you think this is foolhardy and that you should just watch, then go to **Decision 256**.

381

Cautiously Harder's men begin to move forward. Suddenly a sheet of small arms and machine-gun fire pins the advance. You have seriously underestimated the strength of the enemy. From the fire being laid down there must be four- or five-times more British paratroopers dug in around the bridge than you had possibly expected. To add to the confusion, Dutch civilians are running for their lives, many of them are cut down in the crossfire. The enemy is not going to give in easily; this is going to be a hard battle. If you want to persevere with the attack you should turn to **Decision 233**. If you want to call it off until morning then go to **Decision 382**.

382

0600 hours 18 September 18 944

During the night you hear that the 10th SS has moved towards the ferry crossing at Pannerden. They hope that they will be able to cross here and then approach Nijmegen from the east, as you have ordered. You make the decision to look closely at the defences around Arnhem Bridge and to try to judge the strength of the enemy that has already dug in around those positions.

'Sir, there's armoured movement being reported on the other side of the bridge', Spindler tells you.

Terrible thoughts rush through your mind. It could be the enemy armoured column, but how could they have burst through and overwhelmed Eindhoven and Nijmegen so soon? With great trepidation you raise your binoculars and try to make out the vehicles. You stare for several seconds, trying to figure out what you are watching.

'I think its Graebner', you tell Spindler.

'You're right, he's going to try to rush the bridge!' Spindler replies.

If you want to launch an immediate attack on the northern side of the bridge to support him then go to **Decision 253**. If you prefer to leave the glory to him then go to **Decision 359**.

383

'Hold them Spindler! Keep pressing to help Graebner, this is the key moment!' you shout.

The situation is critical. Graebner's attack is floundering and the British reinforcements are flooding into the streets. Already you can see knots of SS troopers throwing down their weapons. Black, acrid smoke covers the whole area. The intensity of the fire is ruinous and Spindler's command is disintegrating. If you want to continue to resist you should go to **Decision 342**. If you want to order a withdrawal, go to **Decision 323**.

384

British machine guns are finding the range of your position. The bullets spark and whine off the metal of your staff car. Some of the troopers are still trying to get forward but most of them are now breaking and abandoning everything in their desperate attempts to escape the carnage. Out of the corner of your eye you see Spindler literally disappear as a mortar round lands close by. You feel a blast and you are knocked off your feet. Your head is swimming and your ears ringing. At first you think it is your driver crouched over you, offering you a flask of water. The man holds your neck up so you can drink. Then you notice the uniform; it is khaki and he is wearing a red beret.

'You're safe now chum', the soldier tells you.

You are a prisoner of war and your command of the operation is at an end.

385

'Stop Graebner, we're too close! The enemy is in too great a strength, far more than we could have imagined', you tell him.

'Call off the attack?' he questions.

'No, you must press on. But I cannot be risked', you reply.

With great difficulty the armoured car reverses, narrowly avoiding oncoming half-tracks. The intensity of the fire is shocking and the men seem to be riding to their deaths. Graebner deposits you beyond the summit of the bridge, salutes and then speeds forward to lead his men to glory. Now turn to **Decision 324**.

386

2400 hours 18 September 1944

Your visit to the southern side of the Waal has not allayed your fears about the dangers to Nijmegen. Corps Feldt is wholly under-strength to mount determined attacks on the Americans. There is better news at Nijmegen; Reinhold's men have arrived and a strong line of defence has been set up. Mines are being laid and even now artillery is firing into the American landing area. The enemy is replying with mortar fire. There are unconfirmed reports that enemy armour has been spotted approaching Nijmegen from the south-west. Now turn to **Decision 304**.

387

1600 hours 19 September 1944

To your horror you learn that there are rumours of British tanks in the outskirts of Nijmegen. The American paratroopers are also on the move and are believed to have penetrated the centre of the town. This is a very worrying development. If you want to order all units to withdraw over the bridge and seek permission to blow the bridges then you should turn to **Decision 236**. If you want to belatedly push reinforcements across the bridges to hold a firm perimeter, go to **Decision 364**.

388

'Field Marshal, I submit that the bridges are under direct threat and request permission to use my own initiative to destroy them', you ask.

You hold the radio set, tensely waiting for Model's reply. Clearly he is thinking about the situation.

'No Bittrich! If you cannot hold your nerve then I will replace you. Do you understand me?' he tells you. 'I will not countenance the destruction of the Nijmegen bridges.'

If you want to argue with him go to **Decision 325**. If you think he is right after all you should turn to **Decision 237**.

389

1800 hours 20 September 1944

As you speed north towards Elst you are cheered by the sight of Captain Knaust and his command making their way south. You stop him and he quickly explains that the Arnhem Bridge is secure. The knot of enemy paratroopers at the bridge has been overwhelmed. Following Knaust is what remains of Graebner's reconnaissance unit. It seems that they have arrived in the nick of time. Something can now be done to hold back the enemy thrust out of Nijmegen. The question is whether to hold the line between Nijmegen and Arnhem, or to fall back and create a defensive perimeter around the Arnhem Bridge. If you want to form a line here, go to **Decision 286**. If you want to order a defensive ring around the southern approach to the bridge, go to **Decision 366**.

390

You strike south, crossing the Ede-Arnhem railway, to the west of Wolfheze. Ahead of you there is some movement.

'I don't like this general', your driver tells you.

'What is it? What did you see?' you urge.

'I'm not sure, but I think whoever they were they've just dived into cover', your driver replies.

If you want to tell your driver to continue, go to **Decision 260**. If you want to turn back and rejoin the units near the enemy landing zones you should go to **Decision 217**.

391

'Fall back towards Arnhem. Inform all units to dig in on the outskirts of the town and establish a link with our blocking line to the south', you order your officers.

Units begin moving, but it is a perilous retreat, with the enemy close on your trail. Von Tettau will have to continue to press from the west. Providing you can hold the northern and north-east routes into Arnhem you can still feed in reinforcements and force the bridge. Once this has been achieved you can then focus on dealing with the isolated enemy paratrooper units on the north of the Rhine. Now turn to **Decision 239**.

392

1800 hours 19 September 1944

A quick visit to the bridgehead area confirms that your men are doing everything to reduce the enemy pocket, but they still resist. Time is running out; Nijmegen must be reinforced, but the 10th SS is still not in a position to get there in force. You need to take the bridge by the end of the day. You order Harzer and his assembled officers to make all necessary preparations. With grim determination, the officers brief their units. They send them into the inferno that is the bridgehead. Still the enemy resists, desperately fighting for every square metre of the perimeter. By midnight your men are bloodied and beaten once again. Their strength is spent. You now discover that renewed attacks by the rest of the enemy force to the west have punched through your defence line in several places. It looks as if Arnhem will be lost. Now turn to **Decision 262**.

393

1915 hours 20 September 1944

It is Harmel that contacts you first. 'General, Nijmegen is lost, both bridges. I ordered their destruction but the charges failed', he begins.

'My God!' you exclaim.

'The bizarre thing is that the enemy has stopped; they are not advancing', he continues.

'What do you mean stopped?'

'Just that. I can't explain it.'

'I'm coming. I'll be in Elst before midnight', you tell him.

With the situation nearly under control here at Arnhem you make your way east then cross the Pannerden Canal. It is nearly 0100 hours the next day before you reach Elst. During the journey the enemy has been beaten at the Arnhem bridgehead. This gives you fresh hope and resolve. Already German troops are flooding south. When you get to Elst you can see that it is true; the enemy has not advanced.

If you want to establish your lines here, go to **Decision 286**. If you want to fall back and set up a defence perimeter around Arnhem Bridge you should turn to **Decision 366**.

394

'I respectfully submit my resignation, Field Marshal. Clearly you have no faith in me any more.'

'Everyone makes mistakes Bittrich, even me. Perhaps I was wrong to put my confidence in you.'

'I think that is unfair, Field Marshal. The odds have been against us from the beginning.'

'Perhaps, but has it not been this way so many times? I accept your resignation. I will take personal command for the time being. Report to Berlin', he finishes.

Your military career is over and you can only guess what the future might hold.

395

1200 hours 24 September 1944

Enemy troop build-ups on the opposite side of the river at Driel are continuing. Intelligence suggests that the bulk of a British infantry division is poised to cross the river. This is very disquieting news. This may be your last chance to settle the issue. If you want to order an all out attack on the enemy north of the river, go to **Decision 350**. If you want to continue to press, go to **Decision 223**.

396

0600 hours 25 September 1944

Shortly before midnight the British commander of the forces on the northern bank requested time to consult with senior officers. Another message was received at 0400, requesting a ceasefire and negotiations. Jubilant, you drive along the main road out of Arnhem to meet the enemy commander, Urquhart, to formally accept his surrender. It seems that hostilities on the northern bank are already dying down. Columns of ambulances are already evacuating the wounded. The final victory is yours, but at a terrible cost. The loss of the ground between Nijmegen and Arnhem is disastrous and cannot be regained without extreme loss of life. You know that the enemy will now consolidate, move up to the Rhine in force and then engineer a crossing elsewhere. Time is running out for Germany.

397

0600 hours 25 September 1944

Your worst fears are realised when you are given reports that the enemy has reinforced the bridgehead, with at least one fresh division of infantry. The lead elements of the 9th SS are being broken by intense artillery fire. There is an unconfirmed report that suggests that a Bailey bridge has been virtually completed and is running alongside the ferry crossing. There is also a steady traffic of assault boats crossing and re-crossing the Rhine. You have hesitated at the last. You know your troops will not be able to hold the line at Oosterbeek under such enormous pressure. In a matter of hours Arnhem itself will be under threat. Your forces to the south of the Rhine face being cut off. You have been outwitted and outmanoeuvred. Your next conversation with Field Marshal Model is not going to be an easy one.

398

2100 hours 25 September 1944

You receive news that shortly before 2000 elements of the 9th SS have established contact with von Tettau's forces in the west. They have broken through close to the river, cutting the enemy off from reinforcement on the south bank of the Rhine. Now you can hear a massive barrage of artillery from the southern bank and you wonder what is in store next. Now turn to **Decision 399**.

399

2300 hours 25 September 1944

You drive towards Oosterbeek to personally organise the last plans of the attacks. You can see the gun flashes in the darkness. It is a stormy night, with torrential rain and heavy winds. As you approach the edge of the enemy perimeter you see columns of British paratroopers. Many of them are wounded and they are being herded west, towards Arnhem. You think it ironic that they will see Arnhem as prisoners of war when they expended so much blood trying to take it as an all-conquering army.

'What's happening at the river?' you demand, finding Harzer directing more attacks.

'I think they intended to evacuate tonight. We cut them off at the last minute', he tells you, grinning.

'Excellent, mop up here. You are needed south. Field Marshal Model has plans for the corps', you tell him.

Very few of the enemy manage to escape; barely 1,000 by your reckoning. The whole British airborne division has been shattered and thousands are either dead, wounded or prisoners. The allies will have to think again if they want to break through to Germany.

400

2300 hours 25 September 1944

Wind, rain and constant artillery fire in the darkness makes it nearly impossible to work out what is happening. Scattered reports along the perimeter suggest that resistance is slackening and your men are moving forward again.

'Fire a flare', you order, pointing at the river.

Illuminated by the flare you can see countless assault boats. At first you fear it is an invasion force. Another flare lights the darkness again and you realise the assault boats are empty. It is no attack; it is an evacuation. You order your units to fire on the assault boats, but they keep coming, ferrying out enemy paratroopers from the ever shrinking perimeter.

You personally conduct operations until dawn. The threat to the Rhine is finished for now. Some 10,000 enemy paratroopers landed north of the Rhine; at least three-quarters of them are either dead, wounded or prisoners of war. It has been a bloody victory for Germany, with at least 15,000 killed or wounded. The strike at the heart of the Reich has been foiled, but it will only be a matter of time before another is launched.